Tricks of the Writer's Trade

What links Cinderella to Harry Potter? What can *The Simpsons* teach us about character creation? What is the False Horizon moment? What are the two classic openings and five effective endings of a newspaper story? Aimed at primary and early secondary school teachers, *Tricks of the Writer's Trade* uses a simple, straightforward and highly entertaining method to reveal a myriad of writing approaches, from basic story structure through to advanced scriptwriting, and the techniques used by professional writers and journalists.

Covering fiction and non-fiction writing, chapters include guidance on:

- story structure;
- creating characters;
- persuasive writing;
- informative writing;
- scriptwriting;
- writing techniques.

By following its step-by-step approach and using the resources and materials provided, teachers can engage their pupils, dramatically improve their writing skills – and have fun while they're doing it. Writing lessons will never be the same again!

Tricks of the Writer's Trade is an invaluable resource for all primary teachers, Key Stage 3 English teachers and literacy coordinators as well as PGCE students.

Rick Vanes is a writer, journalist and educational consultant in the UK. Having been a professional writer for more than 40 years, he has written scripts for over 2000 television programmes; six children's books; hundreds of press stories for local and national newspapers; and training and information material for major businesses and organisations. His website can be found at www.rickvanes.co.uk.

Tricks of the Writer's Trade

And how to teach them to children aged 8–14

Rick Vanes

Routledge
Taylor & Francis Group

LONDON AND NEW YORK

First published 2012
by Routledge
2 Park Square, Milton Park, Abingdon, Oxon OX14 4RN

Simultaneously published in the USA and Canada
by Routledge
711 Third Avenue, New York, NY 10017

Routledge is an imprint of the Taylor & Francis Group, an informa business

British Library Cataloguing in Publication Data
A catalogue record for this book is available from the British Library

Library of Congress Cataloging in Publication Data
Vanes, Rick.
Tricks of the writer's trade : and how to teach them to children aged 8–14 / Rick
Vanes.
p. cm.
Includes bibliographical references and index.
1. Composition (Language arts) I. Title.
LB1575.8.V364 2012
372.62'3–dc23
2011021778

ISBN: 978-0-415-67777-6 (hbk)
ISBN: 978-0-415-67779-0 (pbk)
ISBN: 978-0-203-80807-8 (ebk)

Typeset in Bembo
by FiSH Books, Enfield

Printed and bound in Great Britain by
TJ International Ltd, Padstow, Cornwall

Contents

Acknowledgements   *vi*
Introduction   *1*

Part 1 Fiction   **5**
  1   Basic story structure   7
  2   Back Story and first exercise in writing   19
  3   How to get ideas for stories   27
  4   Creating believable characters   35
  5   Writing a story   44
  6   Rewriting   51

Part 2 Non-fiction   **55**
  7   Non-fiction writing – an overview   57
  8   Writing to inform/journalism   64
  9   Persuasive writing I – the poster   73
 10   Persuasive writing II – the essay   83

Part 3 Fiction – advanced   **89**
 11   Advanced character creation   91
 12   Advanced structure   100
 13   Scriptwriting   109
 14   Advanced scriptwriting   114

Part 4 Non-fiction – advanced   **121**
 15   Advanced non-fiction techniques   123

Teacher resources   *130*
Index   *146*

Acknowledgements

I would like to thank:

Jacob Brown for providing me with the story about his athletics success and for letting me use it in this book.

Rick Whittaker, head teacher of Allerton Grange School in Leeds, for allowing me to use the stories I wrote for the school magazine as a teaching resource.

Helen Patmore and Allison Jolly of Witham St Hughs Primary School in Lincoln – it was while hosting workshops with them that I was inspired to write this book.

Nicola Towle of Fulford School in York . . . and all the other teachers I have worked with over the years who have helped me with comments and advice. I am grateful to you all.

Introduction

The first thing to say is that I'm not a teacher – at least, I never trained as one. I'm a full-time professional writer and have been since the age of 18 (which is a long time ago!), writing for newspapers, magazines, television, books and videos. I write fiction and non-fiction, prose and scripts, for children and adults.

For the past 15 years or so, while continuing to work as a writer, I have also spent a lot of time in schools, teaching children how to write. In order to do this, I had to think long and hard about what I actually *did* when I sat down at the keyboard: what my thought processes were and what techniques I used – things that I did instinctively, without really thinking about them.

The challenge then was to devise entertaining and effective ways of teaching them to children – and over the years I refined and developed the content of the workshops and my methods for putting them across, learning a great deal from teachers along the way. For example, after one day of workshops in which I worked with five different year groups, and, therefore, did not have a great deal of time to spend with each one, the feedback I got afterwards revealed that, while the children had really enjoyed and benefited from the content, they felt that they hadn't been allowed sufficient time to actually write. It was a valuable lesson for me, and one from which I learned (as, hopefully, will the teachers and workshop leaders who use this book).

I also learned from teachers the value of encouraging children to read out their stories for appraisal by their classmates. This was something I didn't do in my early days of hosting workshops – and really, I should have known better. *All* writers, no matter how experienced and celebrated they might be, enjoy putting their work before an audience and basking in praise. That's a fundamental reason why most of us began writing in the first place!

Apart from a couple of useful exercises in vocabulary expansion and the avoidance of repetition, and some tips on writing style, there is not a great deal in this book about the teaching of English Language; that's something that teachers know how to do already. What I concentrate on are things that teachers may well not be familiar with – things like story structure, ways of injecting drama, character creation, etc. – the things that writers need to know, but most other people don't.

When giving examples from stories to illustrate various points, I refer not just to books, but also films and TV – things which, as teachers know only too well, many children prefer to the printed page. Whether we approve or disapprove of that is beside the point; it is a fact. And looking on the positive side, it means that children who only know *The Lord of the Rings* and Harry Potter through the films, rather than the books, are still familiar with the story – so we can refer to them in the knowledge that the children will know what we are talking about. At the end of the day, books, films, plays, TV programmes and newspaper articles all have something in common: they are all telling stories in one form or another. And in reading or watching those stories – whatever type they may be – children will learn something useful. If they have been taught the professional writing techniques outlined in this book, they will be able to identify structural elements such as Inciting Incidents, obstacles, False Horizon moments and the different ways of beginning and ending a piece of writing; they will become more familiar with them – and that will benefit their own writing.

A word of warning, though: among the things they watch and read, there will be examples of good writing and bad. Even professional writers get it wrong sometimes – but, hopefully, children who have absorbed all the information given in this book will not only be able to recognise that it isn't very good, but also be able to pinpoint some of the reasons why it doesn't work as well as it could. Well, it's possible, at any rate!

How should this book be used? Well, that's entirely up to you, of course. You may be planning to put on a series of half-day or full-day workshops, or you may want to use the material in weekly lessons. Your priority may be fiction or non-fiction, or you may wish to give equal attention to both. In my workshops, I have used the material in all sorts of combinations and for a wide variety of age-groups, so hopefully you should have no problem in putting together a package of lessons that meet your needs exactly. But whichever route you choose to go down, there are some important things to bear in mind:

When teaching fiction writing, the workshop on story structure in Chapter 1 is an essential starting point. Without knowing something about how stories are put together, the chances of young people becoming accomplished writers will be very much reduced. Similarly, the information given in Chapter 8 about non-fiction intros and endings is crucial; it is something that they will be able to use effectively in many different forms of writing.

The importance of those chapters is reflected in the fact that I have written them almost as a step-by-step guide to running a workshop or lesson and I have done the same with other crucial elements which form the basis of good writing, such as character creation or the art of writing persuasively. Chapters which deal with more advanced techniques are written slightly less prescriptively, making it easier for teachers to tailor them to their specific requirements.

And some adaptation *will* probably be required. The material in this book is suitable for 8–14 year olds (although it will be useful for older students, too – not to mention adults!), and the average Year 4 pupil has little in common with a hulking teenager. But teachers should find it relatively straightforward to switch things around a little to make the lessons more appropriate for their pupils.

For example, if you are teaching fiction writing to older, slightly cynical, maybe even disaffected young people, I would not recommend launching straight into the Cinderella exercise, even though it is absolutely crucial to the understanding of structure. Instead, try starting with the 'Unexpected' technique for getting story ideas, which is covered in Chapter 3. Involve them in getting the 'flood' scenario under way, which they will probably find pretty engaging, and then break off by saying something along the lines of: 'If we were writing this as a movie, we'd need to know something about structure in order to make it as exciting as possible – so let's look at how lots of stories, including most films, are put together …' and then run the Cinderella exercise without getting them to play the various roles (which they would probably object to!). Once you've covered the basics of the Obstacles Structure, you can then return to the flood story, point out that the water gushing in is the Inciting Incident and then discuss the journey and obstacles.

The chapters on advanced fiction and non-fiction writing explain the principles to be taught to young people once they have mastered the basics and are ready to develop their skills further. The age at which children will be ready to move on to these more advanced techniques will vary widely, depending on their ability. Some may be ready at primary school, others may never be ready but will content themselves with using just the basic principles. And there's nothing wrong with that – even if they have only mastered simple structures and techniques, they will still be pretty capable writers.

The resources provided in the Teacher resources section at the back of the book should prove extremely useful – I know *I* couldn't run my workshops without them – and you will find they are easily adaptable to meet your specific requirements. For example, the Who Is This Character? – Boy and Who Is This Character? – Girl documents feature photographs of children aged about 12; if you felt that photographs of younger or older children, or maybe adults, would be more appropriate for the class you are teaching, then it would be very straightforward to create new resources based on the ones provided, but using different photos.

This book is a distillation of all the things I have learned in a lifetime of writing, and I hope you find it useful. The ideas and methods contained in it are not theoretical – they have all been tried and tested over many years and have been instrumental in helping an awful lot of young people become better writers. I trust they'll prove successful for you, too.

Basic story structure

A good way of getting children to think about the importance of structuring a story is by asking them to put their hands up if this has ever happened to them:

> Someone tells you a joke that you think is really funny – but when you tell it to someone else, they don't laugh.

The chances are that a lot of hands will go up; this is something that has happened to most people at one time or another. It can happen because the other person isn't on the same wavelength as you; they may have a different sense of humour; they may have no sense of humour at all – but the most common reason is this:

> You didn't tell the joke very well.

If you don't tell a joke properly, building it step by step until it reaches the punch-line, it's unlikely to produce the desired effect – and the same goes for stories. Whether it's a novel, a short story, a play, a television programme or a film, a story has to be told properly if it is to engage and excite the reader or the audience.

In this chapter we'll be showing the children how to tell a story well by giving it an effective structure. They will learn about:

- the Main Character;
- the Character Journey;
- the need to structure that journey;
- the Obstacles Structure;
- the Inciting Incident;
- the False Horizon.

The lesson will take about one hour and will involve some acting, so a space will need to be cleared at the front of the classroom. Alternatively, the activity could take place in the school hall or some other large room. You will need a whiteboard, smart-board or flip chart on which to draw some basic diagrams.

Using pupils to act out the key events of the Cinderella story is a very effective way of demonstrating how the plot is structured, and one that I have used successfully for all age groups. Younger children thoroughly enjoy it, and even sixth-formers find it fun in a 'retro' sort of way. But 13- and 14-year-olds – young people at an awkward and self-conscious stage of their lives – may not be prepared to play along, in which case the teacher may find it advisable to merely talk through the various stages of the story and reinforce the points being made on the whiteboard.

The Main Character

A story will usually feature a Main Character who drives the story along. This is the protagonist – but since many children will not be familiar with the word, it is advisable at first to call them the 'Main Character' or alternatively 'hero' or 'heroine'. To avoid having to use he/she and his/her all the time, let's assume that our Main Character is female – the heroine.

During the story, she will have a variety of experiences, both good and bad, that will change her in some way. This is what we call a Character Journey.

The Character Journey

Using the word 'journey' tends to make children think of a physical journey from A to B. Indeed, some of the stories they are familiar with will be centred around an actual journey – for example, *The Hobbit* and *The Lord of the Rings*. So how do we explain the concept of a Character Journey to them? For the answer, we turn to reality television.

Most young people will have watched programmes in which the participants try to acquire a new skill, like dancing or ice-skating; they will have seen TV talent shows and programmes that involve people facing various challenges. When the participants are voted off the show, they will often talk about what an 'amazing journey' it has been, meaning that they have had some memorable experiences and learned something from them. Ask children if they are familiar with this use of the word 'journey' and you will probably find that most of them are. In other words, they already know what a Character Journey is.

Another way of explaining the concept is to get the children to think about their own lives. As new-born babies, they were helpless and couldn't do anything for themselves, but over the years they have learned to walk, talk and think; they have acquired knowledge, had lots of different experiences and developed their own individual personalities. The things that have happened to them in their lives will have shaped the way that they are now – and the same is true of a character in a story.

The Character Journey for our hero or heroine will usually lead to a goal or a variety of goals, for example:

- love;
- happiness;
- knowledge;
- righting a wrong;
- escape;
- success (as a musician, writer, actor, sports star);
- treasure (*The Hobbit*);
- fulfilment of a destiny (Harry Potter);
- or it could be a journey to find a person (murder suspect, missing person, birth parent).

But whatever the goal is, by the end of the journey our heroine will have changed because of what she has experienced – and the change could be for the better or for the worse. She may be:

- happier;
- sadder;
- richer;
- poorer;
- loved;
- hated;
- fulfilled;
- frustrated.

And she will probably know more at the end than she did at the beginning. Whether she has succeeded or failed in reaching her goal, she will probably be wiser.

If our readers are to become involved in a character's journey, *they must identify with her* and want her to succeed in reaching her goal. We can achieve this in various ways:

- By giving our characters attractive personality traits – kind, funny, brave, honest, independent, determined, quirky, well-meaning, etc.

- By giving them some special talent that we envy and admire – they may be good at sport, art, music or dancing; they may have a strong affinity with animals; they may be able to do magic or possess super-powers.

- By making them outsiders – people who don't really fit in with everybody else and are different in some way; people we may sympathise with or who intrigue us. Think how many books feature children who are orphans; think how many TV detectives are odd-balls who never play it by the book.

The structure of 'Cinderella'

Now let's look at how some of these elements fit together in a story which everybody knows – Cinderella. Any groans from older children who may consider Cinderella a little babyish usually disappear when they are told that, at the end of the lesson, you will show them how the structure of this story corresponds closely with the early chapters of the first Harry Potter book!

There are different versions of Cinderella: the original story by Charles Perrault, the 1950 Walt Disney film, and any number of pantomimes. Each tells the story in a slightly different way; for example, in many pantomimes, Cinderella's father is still alive and the character of Buttons plays a significant role. However, the version that most children know best is the Disney film, so that is the best one to use. It begins with a brief narrative giving the back story: Cinderella's mother died; her father re-married; then he died, too, and Cinderella was left at the mercy of her Wicked Stepmother and the two Ugly Sisters.

The first question to ask the children is a straightforward one:

Who is the Main Character?

When a forest of hands goes up, I usually choose a girl to answer the question, so that her 'reward' for answering correctly is that she gets to play the part of Cinderella in our reconstruction of the story. Our Cinderella is now brought out to the front as we discuss her role in the story.

The next questions to deal with are:

Why do we care about Cinderella? What makes her a sympathetic character?

Children will usually come up with a variety of reasons: she's being bullied; she's an orphan; she's kind, sweet, beautiful, gentle, etc. These character traits are established in a scene very early in the film, in which birds and mice come to greet Cinderella when she wakes up. If the woodland creatures love her, she must be a nice person! It's important to stress that, despite being such a lovely girl, she has an unhappy home life – because this will help the children to answer the next questions:

What is Cinderella's journey? What is her goal?

To help the children with this, it may be necessary to refer them back to the examples of goals given earlier. From that list, three would probably fit the bill for Cinderella: happiness, love and escape from drudgery.

Much easier is the final question:

How can she achieve her goal?

The obvious solution is by marrying Prince Charming, and you should try to get a boy to give the answer so that you have a 'volunteer' to play this role. Bring him out to the front and place him on the opposite side of the room from Cinderella.

So now we have our Main Character and her goal with a gap between them – and that gap is going to be filled by the story we are about to tell. It is a good idea to draw a simple diagram on the whiteboard to reinforce this:

CINDERELLA  PRINCE CHARMING

If she simply meets the Prince in the street, they fall in love and she marries him, it would be a pretty boring story – but we could make it exciting if we placed obstacles in Cinderella's path as she moves towards her goal. These could be problems that she has to solve, disappointments that she encounters or people who are trying to prevent her from achieving her goal. They keep our audience involved with the story as they ask themselves: how will she deal with this problem? Will she or won't she succeed? What's going to happen next?

For the purposes of this book, we're going to give this a self-explanatory name – the Obstacles Structure – and we can show the class how it works by placing obstacles on our diagram:

Children find the concept easy to grasp when told that it's just like a hurdles race, with the runners having to leap over a series of obstacles before they reach the finishing line:

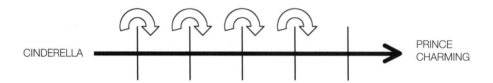

But before we start to put the story together, let's consider one problem: Cinderella is stuck in the house, busy all day with her chores, and the Prince is in his palace. The two of them are not likely to meet, so we have to find a way of bringing that about.

In a hurdles race, a starting pistol is fired to set the runners off – and a story needs the equivalent of that. Something needs to happen that will launch our Main Character on her journey, and this event is known as the Inciting Incident.

So what is the Inciting Incident in the story of Cinderella? What happens that gives her the opportunity of meeting the Prince? The first child to come up with the correct answer – *the invitation to the ball* – should be given a piece of paper, representing a ticket, and asked to give it to Cinderella. So now her journey can begin and we are ready to place the obstacles.

It's fun – and effective – to have children acting out the obstacles. They stand in Cinderella's way, blocking her route to the Prince, and each time an obstacle is overcome she walks past the child who represents it, bringing her a little closer to her goal.

The first obstacle she faces is:

She's not allowed to go to the ball.

To demonstrate this we select two boys to play the Ugly Sisters (boys love playing those parts and tend to bring a lot of energy to their roles!) plus a girl to play the Wicked Stepmother. We get the Ugly Sisters to stand directly in front of Cinderella and tell her:

> '*You're* not going!'

So how do we get around this obstacle? In the Disney film, the Wicked Stepmother says that Cinderella can go if she finishes all her work in time, but then gives her an enormous number of chores to do. This means that, even if she manages to do all the jobs, she won't have time to make herself a ball gown.

Her friends the mice rally round and make her a dress, using lace and ribbons 'borrowed' from the Ugly Sisters – but just when it seems that Cinderella can go to the ball after all, the Ugly Sisters claim back their possessions, leaving her dressed in rags. The sisters and the Wicked Stepmother leave for the ball, so the obstacle that they represent is removed and Cinderella can move forward slightly, but she is still unable to go to the ball because of the next obstacle:

> She can't go dressed in rags.

We represent this by selecting a child to act as a fashion expert, standing in front of Cinderella and telling her:

> 'You can't go dressed like that!'

How is Cinderella going to surmount this obstacle? Children don't need much prompting to come up with the solution – the Fairy Godmother. By selecting a girl to answer this question, we have a ready-made Fairy Godmother. Giving her a ruler or board marker to represent a wand adds to the fun, and when she waves it over Cinderella, turning her rags into a beautiful ball gown, our heroine can move forward past the obstacle. But now she's presented with another problem:

> How will she get to the ball?

A child playing our transport expert represents this obstacle by blocking Cinderella's path and saying:

> 'It's too far to walk!'

Again, the Fairy Godmother comes to the rescue by waving her wand and turning a pumpkin into a coach, mice into horses and a dog into a footman. So Cinderella can move forward past the obstacle and join the Prince at the ball.

Her journey seems to be complete, but is it? Of course not – ending the story here would be pretty boring, so we add some drama and excitement by placing another obstacle:

The magic ends at midnight.

A child playing the role of a clock and chiming 'Bong! Bong!' causes Cinderella to panic and as she hurries away from the Prince and back to her starting position, we describe her dress turning back into rags and her coach back into a pumpkin, etc. So now we are back where we began, with Cinderella at home in rags and the Prince in his palace; there is still a large gap between them. It seems that her journey has ended in failure, because she couldn't get over the last obstacle.

At this point, it's helpful to return to the diagram on the whiteboard, make the line that represents the last obstacle thicker and higher, and give it a special name: the False Horizon.

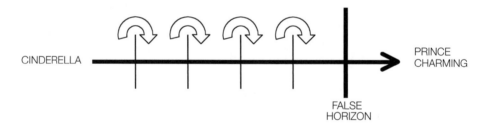

It's that dramatic moment which is often to be found in stories, when characters think they have succeeded in something – only for success to be snatched away at the last moment. The reason why I refer to it as the False Horizon is because it is easy to illustrate to children by means of the following diagram:

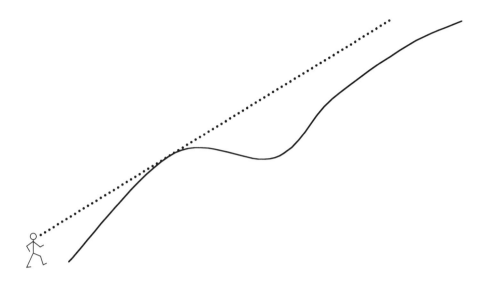

It represents a man who plans to climb to the top of a hill. He sees what he *thinks* is the top of the hill, but when he reaches it he will find that he has only completed the first part of his climb. The hill goes on and on, but he can't see that from where he is standing. What he thinks is the top of the hill is just a False Horizon.

A very good example of a False Horizon – and one that most children are familiar with – is to be found in *The Lord of the Rings*. Frodo's journey is to put the Ring beyond the reach of Sauron and he believes that if he takes it to the elves in Rivendell, they will keep it safe. He has to overcome lots of obstacles to get there, but when he arrives, and thinks that he has fulfilled his task, he learns that the Ring won't be safe in Rivendell after all. It must be taken to Mount Doom and destroyed – and of course Frodo is the one who has to take it there. He has many more dangers ahead before he succeeds in his mission; Rivendell was only a False Horizon.

Returning to the story of Cinderella, we witnessed one False Horizon moment early on in the piece, when the mice made a dress for our heroine. She believed that she was going to be the belle of the ball, only to see her hopes dashed when the Ugly Sisters tore up her dress. And now she has come to a second, and even more devastating, False Horizon with the chiming of the clock at midnight. She was on the verge of completing her journey, only for the prospect of love and happiness to be snatched away at the last moment.

We still want to bring her and the Prince together, but how are we going to achieve that? We don't want to send her on the same journey again, but what we can do is turn things around.

Act 1 of the story was Cinderella's journey towards the Prince, but Act 2 will be about the Prince's journey towards Cinderella. Since we have already established the principles of the Inciting Incident, the obstacles and the False Horizon, there is no need to deal with the events of Act 2 in such great detail; a quick run-through with a minimum of acting will suffice.

We need an Inciting Incident to set him off on his journey and the children should have no trouble in identifying it:

Prince Charming finds the glass slipper.

Now we need some obstacles to place in his way. The first one is:

He doesn't know who she is or where she lives.

The solution is to let every lady in the land try the slipper on. (The fact that it will only fit Cinderella's foot is very handy!) He finally reaches Cinderella's house, but here there is another obstacle:

Cinderella has been locked in her room.

In the Disney film, this obstacle is overcome by the mice, who steal the key to her room with the intention of letting her out. They have to deal with a couple more obstacles – the cat who is trying to stop them and a steep flight of stairs that they have difficulty in climbing – but eventually, and at the very last minute, they succeed in freeing Cinderella.

In this version of the story, she doesn't actually get to try on the slipper, since the Wicked Stepmother contrives to smash it – another obstacle – but fortunately Cinderella manages to produce the matching slipper, proving that she is the mystery girl that the Prince fell in love with.

And so Cinderella's journey has ended successfully and she and the Prince can live happily ever after.

The Obstacles Structure is a fairly common one and by following the basic steps children have a clear template for writing their own stories:

1. Create a Main Character that the reader can identify with and care about.
2. Decide what that character's journey will be.
3. Think of an Inciting Incident to set your character off on that journey.
4. Place obstacles that make the journey more exciting.
5. Try to add one or more False Horizon moments for added drama.

Children should be encouraged to think about books and films that they enjoy and try to identify Inciting Incidents, obstacles and False Horizons, to reinforce how effective they are in telling a story.

Something that children find fascinating is the way in which the opening chapters of the first Harry Potter book – *Harry Potter and the Philosopher's Stone* – closely mirror many of the elements we have dealt with in Cinderella. Most children know the book very well and will be able to spot the similarities when you ask them the following questions:

> Why do we care about Harry Potter?

He's an orphan who is mistreated by his uncle, aunt and cousin – some pretty strong parallels there!

> What is Harry's Character Journey?

Children tend to come up with a variety of suggestions: to fulfil his destiny; to become a wizard; to save the world; to kill Voldemort; to avenge his parents; to escape an unhappy home life. Harry's journey is a multifaceted one.

> What is the Inciting Incident that launches Harry's journey?

The letters inviting him to Hogwarts – just like Cinderella's invitation to the ball.

And the similarities continue as obstacles are placed in his way: his family want to prevent him from going; he needs the right equipment – although in his case that means robes, a wand, broomstick, etc., rather than a ball gown; he is helped to get what he needs by Hagrid, acting as his Fairy Godmother; Cinderella needed transport to get to the ball and Harry needs to catch the Hogwarts Express.

Whenever the subject of the Hogwarts Express comes up in my workshops, I usually string the children along a little, by saying something along the lines of:

> So he goes along to the station, walks on to the platform and catches the Hogwarts Express …

Invariably I am shouted down and the children insist on explaining to me in great detail how Harry needs to run through a brick wall in order to reach the platform – and that provides me with a golden opportunity to reinforce the structure they have been learning about:

A brick wall? How good an obstacle is that!

Once they are made aware of Inciting Incidents, obstacles and False Horizon moments, children usually get a lot of satisfaction out of spotting examples of them in the books that they read or the films and television programmes that they watch. It makes them feel as if they are in on a secret that not many people know: the author is using a writer's trick to make the story more exciting and *they* have spotted what he or she is up to.

This is to be encouraged – because the more familiar they become with structural techniques, the more they will start to think like writers and the better their writing will become. It could even be a homework assignment: 'Watch a film over the weekend and try to spot one Inciting Incident, two obstacles and a False Horizon moment.'

Now *that's* a piece of homework that not many of them would grumble about!

2

Back Story and first exercise in writing

Having learned how stories are put together, the children should be ready (and hopefully eager!) to use the principles of the Obstacles Structure in creating a story of their own. The lesson will require the use of a whiteboard, smart-board or flip chart on which to draw a diagram, and by the end of it the children will have produced the 'outline' of a story.

They will be asked to create their own sequel to the Cinderella story – Cinderella II, if you like – but before they begin to plan their stories, they need to learn about something called …

Back Story

In order to explain what Back Story is, let's look at Cinderella's life. As with all lives, it's a journey from birth through to death, which we can illustrate by this simple diagram:

B ▬▬▬▬▬▬▬▬▬▬▬▬▬▬▬▬▬▬▬▬▬▬ D

Certain key events have had a dramatic impact on her – notably the death of her mother, her father's marriage to the Wicked Stepmother, the death of her father, the invitation to the ball and her marriage to the Prince – so let's add them to the diagram:

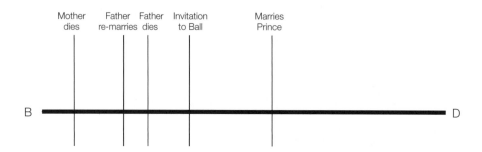

So how has she been affected by those events? We can show that by adding a line which indicates how she is feeling. It's a bit like a temperature chart which rises when she is happy and falls when she is sad and it looks something like this:

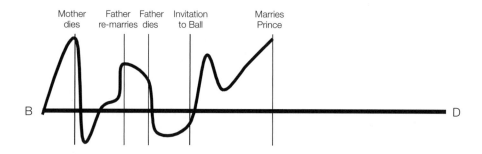

As a baby, she had two loving parents and was very happy – but then her mother died and it must have seemed like the end of the world. She probably thought she would never smile again. But, little by little, she started to get over her mother's death; after all, she still had a father who loved and needed her. She began to enjoy life once more and when her father decided to get married again she was happy for him.

But when her new stepmother and stepsisters moved in, her life took a turn for the worse. Her stepmother continually found fault with her, her step-sisters were conceited and unkind and although she tried to put a brave face on things for her father's sake, she wasn't very happy. And then disaster struck again – her father died, leaving her at the mercy of her stepmother and step-sisters.

Now, Cinderella's father wasn't around to protect her, her stepmother and stepsisters were free to treat her in any way they chose. They could bully her and force her to do all the work and there was nobody to stop them.

It's at this point that our story of Cinderella begins. All the events we have just described – her childhood, the death of her mother, her father's second marriage, his death – have been key elements in shaping Cinderella's character and setting up the situation in which she now finds herself. But they are not things that we have seen happen; we only learn about them as the story progresses.

The story of Cinderella is the shaded section of the diagram below; everything that went before is what we call the **Back Story**:

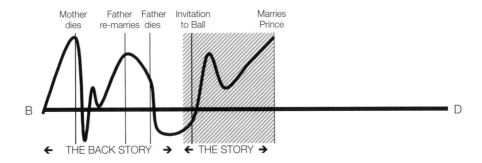

As the diagram illustrates, every story is just one part of a larger story – in this case, the ongoing story of Cinderella's life. Things happened before our story began – the Back Story – and things will happen after the story ends. We're told that after she married the Prince, they both lived happily ever after – but *did* they?

Perhaps the Prince wasn't quite as charming as he seemed. Perhaps the courtiers at the palace thought that a girl who had scrubbed floors wasn't good enough to marry into the Royal Family. Perhaps the Wicked Stepmother and the Ugly Sisters wanted revenge on Cinderella for winning the Prince's heart.

Who knows how Cinderella's story might continue? There are all sorts of possibilities – and now we want the children to explore some of them. If we look at our diagram again, there is a big blank space to be filled in after Cinderella's marriage to the Prince. How might that gap be filled? That's the task facing the children as they start to sketch out their version of Cinderella II – The Sequel.

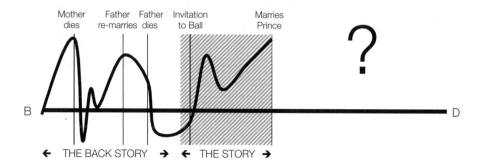

Writing the outline of a story before going on to flesh it out is a good habit for young writers to get into. It encourages them to think the plot through before committing the full version to paper, identifying any weaknesses or places in which the story can be improved. This is what professional writers do; the vast majority of books, TV shows or films will only get commissioned if the author provides an outline first.

So how should the children set about writing their outlines? Well, the first thing to decide upon is the Main Character. Whose story will this be?

They could choose Cinderella as the protagonist – and, no doubt, many of them will. But they could also choose any of the other characters who featured in the original story: Prince Charming; the Wicked Stepmother; the Ugly Sisters; the Fairy Godmother; the King. Or they could introduce a new character: someone at court; a forester who falls in love with Cinderella; the Wicked Stepmother's even wickeder sister; Cinderella's long-lost twin. Perhaps the story might be set a few years after the wedding, in which case the Main Character could be Cinderella's daughter or son.

When they have decided which character they are going to write about, they need to think about the Character Journey. What is their character's goal? What is she trying to achieve? And will she succeed?

What is the Inciting Incident that sets the character off on that journey? What obstacles will she face and how will she get over them? If possible, the story should include a False Horizon moment, when the Main Character thinks she has succeeded, but hasn't.

Writing a check-list on the whiteboard will help the children focus on the key elements that they need to be thinking about:

- Main Character;
- Character Journey;
- Inciting Incident;

- Obstacles;
- False Horizon.

Teachers will have their own ideas on how best to organise this writing exercise – they know their class better than anyone – but in my workshops I usually let the children form themselves into groups of around three or four so that they can collaborate on producing a story outline, with one of them acting as scribe. I usually allow between 10 and 20 minutes for the exercise, depending on the ability of the class.

The outline doesn't have to be too long. If we were sketching one out for the story of Cinderella, it might look something like this:

- Cinderella unhappy – being bullied by stepmother and sisters.
- Invitation to ball – chance to meet Prince Charming (Inciting Incident).
- Obstacles – not allowed to go; dress ruined; needs ball gown, transport.
- Fairy Godmother uses magic to overcome obstacles – new dress, pumpkin turned into coach, animals into footmen, horses, etc.
- Cinderella goes to ball and Prince Charming falls in love with her.
- False Horizon – magic stops at midnight and Cinderella has to flee.
- Prince Charming finds her slipper – whose foot does it fit?
- Tries slipper on all ladies in the land – finally reaches Cinderella's house.
- Stepmother and sisters provide final obstacles – but fail to stop Cinderella trying on slipper. It fits!
- Cinderella and Prince Charming marry.

When they have finished, I get the various groups to share their outlines with the rest of the class, for comment and constructive criticism. This is incredibly useful in helping the children to refine and improve their work; other people's input can be invaluable, as any writer who has attended script conferences with producers and script editors will tell you.

The teacher or workshop leader has an important role to play during the general discussion of the story outlines, gently pointing out any flaws there might be in the logic of the plot. Over the years, I have heard the most fantastical storylines for Cinderella II, involving aliens, vampires, even Britney Spears! However, I am careful not to interfere in the basic concept of the story – if that's what the children choose to write about, then so be it – but I do suggest amendments when the plot defies logic or things happen for no reason.

The three most common flaws to watch out for are:

- A character suddenly displays abilities which we never knew they had.
- Someone behaves completely out of character.
- A character does something for no apparent reason.

To give them technical terms, these are faults in:

- set-up;
- character consistency;
- motivation.

These elements of effective writing are all dealt with in greater detail elsewhere in this book, but, for now, let me give you some examples from my own workshops which illustrate these type of flaws:

Set-up

In one outline I was listening to, Cinderella was being attacked by the Wicked Stepmother, but managed to save herself by using magic to turn her assailant to stone. Very convenient and dramatic – but how come Cinderella can suddenly do magic? It's never been mentioned before; it doesn't make sense.

However – as I suggested to the authors of the outline – supposing we were to add a scene earlier in the piece, in which the Fairy Godmother is teaching Cinderella how to do magic. *Then* it would make sense; we would understand how Cinderella had managed to turn the Wicked Stepmother into a statue, because her ability to do magic had been explained to us. There had been a set-up.

Adding that earlier scene could also provide us with additional possibilities for the story: Cinderella's magic might not always work out as she intended – after all, she's only a beginner, and the Fairy Godmother's command of magic is pretty shaky, given that she can't make it last past midnight. Lots of scope for entertaining scenes there.

Character consistency

In another outline produced in my workshops, the Prince fell in love with one of the Ugly Sisters and they conspired together against Cinderella. From what we know of the Prince and the Ugly Sisters, this would be highly unlikely and totally out of character for the Prince. However, it *would* be believable if the lady in question had managed to slip a love potion into his drink. The Prince's character wouldn't have changed – he'd be behaving in a highly unusual way, but it would be due to circumstances beyond his control.

Motivation

The third example concerned a servant at the palace who stole Cinderella's baby son from his cot and ran off with him – the Character Journey for this particular story being the Prince and Cinderella's quest to find him and get him back. The discovery that the baby had been stolen was a great Inciting Incident, the story was full of obstacles and exciting moments, but the authors failed to answer one vital question: Why did the servant do it? There was no mention of a ransom note, no setting up of the servant's character to show that she was a particularly wicked person – she simply walked into the nursery one day and took the baby. If characters in stories do things for no apparent reason, then we, as readers, feel let down. We want to *know* why people do things; we need to know what their *motivation* is. In this case, it was quite simple to add an extra scene to the story, in which the Wicked Stepmother bribes the servant to steal the baby, and suddenly everything made sense.

There is a common thread running through all three of the flaws mentioned above: in each case, *the authors wrote something because it suited their purpose* and probably seemed like a good idea at the time – but *they didn't stop to consider whether their readers would find it believable.*

This also applies to plots which rely on *coincidence.* If the Prince's long-lost evil twin brother, who was separated from him at birth, just happened to turn up at the Court on the day of the royal wedding, it could lead to very interesting developments. He could be mistaken for the Prince and all sorts of complications could ensue – but would we really be convinced that it was purely by chance that he reappeared on that particular day in that particular place after being missing for 20 years? *I* certainly wouldn't. However, if he had learned of the forthcoming wedding during his travels, and hurried to the kingdom in order to cause mischief and sabotage the big day, then that *would* be believable. The plot would not be relying on coincidence.

Stories ask us to believe all sorts of unlikely things – boy wizards running through walls in order to catch a train, rings that make you invisible, animals that talk – and we *do* believe them, just as long as they make some sort of sense. But if people in stories suddenly acquire special abilities out of the blue, or behave totally out of character, or do things for no reason, or important things happen purely by chance, then their credibility is stretched and the story doesn't engage us.

Teachers and workshop leaders can help children identify and correct these flaws by asking pertinent questions:

- 'How come she can suddenly do magic?'
- 'But what does the Prince *see* in her? She's horrible!'
- 'Why would the servant want to steal the baby?'
- 'That's very convenient – but is it believable?'

In most cases, it only requires a little bit of tweaking to put things right, and with the rest of the class and the teacher throwing ideas into the pot, an effective solution can usually be found.

Armed with story outlines created in this way, children should find writing the story itself a fairly straightforward task. They may well want to get stuck in straightaway, and it might be a good idea to let them, even though there is still plenty for them to learn about such things as making characters believable, where to begin and end a story, etc.

Those will be dealt with in the following chapters, with the emphasis on creating *original* storylines and characters, but for now, writing about situations and characters that they are familiar with would be good practice for them and would help to build up their writing stamina. They're going to need it with all the creative challenges that lie ahead!

3

How to get ideas for stories

There can't be a teacher in the land who hasn't heard this age-old refrain from a child staring at a blank sheet of paper: 'I don't know what to write about!' Well, in this lesson we'll be exploring various ways in which children can address that problem. They will learn about:

- 'Borrowing' ideas from other stories.
- Getting ideas from newspapers.
- Listening to people.
- Being observant.
- Using the 'unexpected' technique.

In my workshops, I usually just talk through the first three bullet points with the children. They don't have a great deal of input, apart from discussing the rights and wrongs of 'borrowing' ideas, but since they are only being asked to sit and listen for a few minutes, it isn't a problem and they will have lots of contributions to make as the workshop progresses.

The section about getting ideas from newspapers can be tackled in one of three ways:

1. Explain the concept to them and provide a couple of examples, before moving on to the next point.
2. Make it an activity, by bringing some newspapers into the classroom and getting the children to look through them in search of story ideas, extending the workshop accordingly.
3. Take option 1 and then use option 2 as a subsequent lesson.

Whichever you choose, the workshop should begin by tackling head on a thorny problem which most teachers of writing are familiar with ...

'Borrowing' ideas

Children are notorious plagiarists – after all, it's easier to pinch someone else's ideas than to go to the trouble of thinking up something original! Obviously, directly copying someone else's story is beyond the pale, but being inspired by an existing story, taking the germ of the idea and running with it, adapting the concept, changing the setting, changing the characters … all this can be an acceptable way to develop a story idea, especially for children who are making their first forays into writing.

Sometimes, writers can find themselves 'borrowing' ideas unwittingly. I certainly have – and you may wish to share this experience of mine with the children: I once read a story in a newspaper about a village school which had so many Traveller pupils that the other parents had started to pull their children out and move them to another school. I thought this might possibly form the basis for a TV drama about Travellers and people's reactions to them and started to think how the story might unfold. In order to show both sides of the argument, I would need a character from each of the two camps … perhaps a teenage boy from the village, whose parents disapproved of the Travellers … and a Traveller girl … and what if they fell in love? … and suddenly I found that I was replicating … (and often, when I tell this story, the children are there ahead of me!) … *Romeo and Juliet*.

If I had written up that idea, would it have been plagiarism? After all, *West Side Story* was based on *Romeo and Juliet* and became hugely successful in its own right. And William Shakespeare is said to have borrowed from earlier sources in writing his play … and when he wrote *King Lear*, he was supposedly inspired by earlier folk tales … and there are parallels between *King Lear* and Cinderella, with the characters of Cinderella and the Ugly Sisters showing marked similarities to Goneril, Regan and Cordelia.

Plagiarism or legitimate 'borrowing'? It's a grey area, but, as far as young writers are concerned, being inspired by other people's stories and putting their own individual slant on it can be a useful starting point. After all, it is said that there are only seven basic plots in the whole of literature!

Getting ideas from newspapers

Newspapers and TV news programmes can be a useful source of story ideas – the Travellers story mentioned above being a good example. Either during this lesson, or a subsequent one, try looking through a few newspapers with the children, to see if any of the articles might form the basis of a story. Local newspapers in particular often contain lots of human interest stories and reports on local issues that can become the starting point for an interesting plot.

For example, you will often find a story about some local campaign against the siting of a mobile phone mast, the closure of a primary school or cottage hospital, the redevelopment of a much-loved building, etc. A campaign is a ready-made journey for a character or characters – maybe a group of children with a social conscience – and with the addition of a villain with a vested interest in opposing the campaign, who is intent on placing obstacles in the children's path, then you have all the ingredients for an exciting story.

One final tip – when looking through your local newspaper for story ideas, don't ignore the Letters page: it usually contains at least one missive from a disgruntled local resident with an axe to grind, and things that make people irate and stir up their emotions can prove to be excellent material for writers in search of a plot!

Listening to people

It's amazing how many ideas for stories you can get by simply listening to other people. At family gatherings, for example, you'll often hear people – particularly the older generation – telling each other stories about things they got up to in their youth; funny, sad or dramatic experiences they have had; stories about relatives who fought in the war, or went to sea, or emigrated to another country, or whatever. It's tempting for children to creep out of the room and go and do something more exciting – but if they were to stay and listen, they might well get enough material for half a dozen stories. The raw materials for stories are all around us – but in order to spot them, we need to keep our eyes and ears open.

Being observant

Writers are usually very observant; they notice things that other people don't, because they're always on the lookout for things that they can turn into a story.

So let's test the children's powers of observation with a game that always proves extremely popular in my workshops: Odd One Out. The premise is simple: I choose three children, either two boys and a girl or two girls and a boy, ask them to stand out in front of the class and then pose the question: 'Which of these three is the odd one out?'

The answer seems straightforward: surely it's the girl standing between two boys? But then I ask the children to look again and see what other differences they can find – and then the fun begins, as other candidates for the position of odd one out start to emerge.

Naturally, the children aren't chosen at random. The girl and one of the boys may be wearing glasses; there may be two with brown hair and one blonde; two with shirts out, one with shirt in; one girl in trousers, one in a skirt, and a boy in trousers. Anything can differentiate one of the children from the other two: colour of top; colour of trousers; colour of shoes; length of hair; variations in school uniform; watches; hair slides; ties; cardigans versus sweaters; lace-up shoes versus slip-ons.

By choosing the three 'volunteers' with care, any number of combinations can be found for the odd one out (usually at least 12) – and the children love trying to spot them. It's a good way of getting the class warmed up and at the same time illustrating an important point:

> What you see at first glance may not be *all* there is to see. So look closely – learn to be observant.

You can practise being observant – and maybe get ideas for stories – every time you make a journey by train, bus or car. All you have to do is look out of the window at the people and places that you are passing by and start to use your imagination:

> Those two men on the corner, muttering to each other – are they spies? That woman who seems in such a hurry – is she late for something? That dog that doesn't seem to have an owner – has it slipped out of the house to go off on an adventure?

Could any of those be used in a story?

Train journeys are particularly useful in this respect, especially if the train is passing through the countryside. From a train window you can see far and wide; during the journey, you might see things like this:

- A big old house in a lonely spot.
- A narrow boat chugging along a canal.
- Someone walking along a country lane.
- A lorry waiting at a level crossing.
- A paddock with show-jumping hurdles made out of old oil cans.
- A scarecrow in a field.

Try to imagine what it might be like to live in a big old house like that – or to travel in a narrow boat. Where is that person on the country lane going to? What is in the lorry and where is it being delivered to? Who does the paddock belong to and what type of horse does he or she have? Who made that scarecrow ... and does it perhaps come to life at night?

Could anything that you see be used in a story? With a little bit of imagination, it almost certainly could. And if you think it might be useful, make a note of it on a piece of paper for future use. Even better, get a notebook and write all your story ideas in it, along with any funny or interesting expressions you might hear. Lots of writers do that – and they find it very useful.

The unexpected

A good piece of advice, which is often given to aspiring writers, is 'Write what you know about.' That's all well and good; we can write more convincingly about things that are familiar to us – our home town, our friends, our everyday lives – than we can about explorers in darkest Africa or astronauts for instance. The problem is that most of the things we are familiar with, most of the things we do every day, can be pretty mundane. You can't write an exciting story about boring everyday things, can you?

Well, actually, you *can* – and you can do it very easily, simply by adding a touch of *the unexpected*. Let's demonstrate how it works by involving the children in the development of a story.

Ask the children what will happen if you open the classroom door. No doubt they'll tell you that you'll find yourself in the corridor or wherever – that's what everyone would expect. But what if the *un*expected happened? What if you opened the door and found yourself in ... a magical world? If this rings bells with the children, and they suggest that you're in Narnia, then they are to be congratulated! Maybe C.S. Lewis got the idea for his stories by asking himself: 'What if a little girl was hiding in a wardrobe, and instead of a wooden panel at the back there was something unexpected ... like branches ... and snow ...'

The Narnia stories have already been written, so let's try something else. What if you opened the door and were knocked off your feet by a great wave of water? This could be the Inciting Incident for a really exciting story, so enlist the children's aid in working it through. If you were to act it out together, then so much the better.

So ... you struggle to your feet and try to close the door, but the pressure of water is too great! You need help – and hopefully the children will come to your aid! Together, you manage to force the door closed – but now you have to ask yourselves some questions:

■ What has happened?

It could be a burst pipe – but there's too much water for that. It must be a flood.

■ You obviously can't get out through that door – so how will you escape?
■ Is there another door?
■ Can you get out of the window?

A story is starting to develop: there has been an Inciting Incident and hopefully the children can identify what the journey is – to escape being drowned in the flood.

If you were to look through the window and see that the flood waters were only a foot or so deep in the playground, you could all climb through the window and escape to safety – but that would be a pretty dull story. It would be as boring as Cinderella simply meeting the Prince in the street, then falling in love and getting married. No – you want the story to be exciting, so you should place obstacles in the way of your escape. What obstacles can the children think of? And how might you overcome those obstacles? Some suggestions might be:

■ The window is locked – but you might be able to smash it. What would you use to break the glass? And would there be a danger of someone getting injured by flying glass?
■ Even if you *do* smash the window, the water outside is very deep. How do you deal with that? Perhaps you could all try to swim to safety – but how dangerous would that be? And can everybody in the class swim? What would happen to the children who can't swim very well?
■ Are there any alternatives to swimming? Could you perhaps build a raft? What with? How would you launch it?
■ Is there a better way of escaping than by getting out through the window? Could you perhaps make your escape upwards? What is the ceiling made of? If it's made of polystyrene tiles, perhaps you could remove some of them and try to get out that way. But how would you get up there? And what might you find if you did – an escape route or a dead end? Might you overcome various obstacles – managing to build a pyramid of desks up to the ceiling, succeeding in prying loose a ceiling tile, etc. – only to

find you'd reached a False Horizon: the cavity above the ceiling is too narrow to squeeze through. What would you do then?

- And meanwhile the flood waters continue to rise …

In this way, by sharing ideas and considering obstacles and ways that you might get around them, an exciting story will start to unfold. It could go in any one of a number of different directions and it all began because when you opened the classroom door, something unexpected happened.

The children may want to write this as a story, or they may want to think of something else that happened unexpectedly when you opened the door and write about that instead. Or perhaps they could write a story based around this scenario, which I use frequently in my workshops:

> I ask if there are two children in the class who are close friends and visit each other's houses regularly to chill out together. In my experience, girls seem to do this more than boys – so let's call our two friends Zoe and Megan.
>
> Zoe invites Megan to call round at 4.30 one afternoon, so they can listen to some music together or watch a DVD – and she can stay for tea if she likes. At 4.30, Megan turns up at Zoe's house, knocks at the door and … a strange woman answers the door. She says that there's no one called Zoe living there … she's never heard of a Zoe … *clear off and don't bother me again.* This is unexpected!
>
> Megan checks the house number – it's the right house. She looks down the street – it's the right street. So what can have happened? Do the children have any suggestions?

The most common one I come across is that Zoe and her family are being held hostage – and we can develop this by having Megan creep round to the back of the house to see if Zoe is in the back garden or yard. Out of the corner of her eye, she thinks she sees a face at a bedroom window – but as she turns to look the face disappears and the curtains are hurriedly drawn. What does she do now? Call the police? Would they take her seriously? Or should she investigate herself?

The latter option is the one that most children take – and quite right, too; it makes for a much better story. But, however they choose to build on the Inciting Incident of the strange woman opening the door, the result should be an interesting and exciting story – and it came about through taking an ordinary, everyday incident, like visiting a friend's house, and adding a touch of the unexpected.

Staring at a blank sheet of paper and hoping that story ideas will come is very rarely productive. But by following the suggestions and techniques described in this chapter, plots and ideas shouldn't be too hard to find. Teach them to your children and hopefully you may never again hear the dreaded words: 'I don't know what to write about!'

And wouldn't that be nice?

CHAPTER

Creating believable characters

Strong characters carry a story along; in engaging with them, the reader engages with the plot. So it's important that the characters in the stories we write should be interesting, realistic – and, above all, *believable*.

In this lesson, we'll be talking through some of the things to consider when creating characters:

- Thinking of characters as real people.
- The importance of names.
- Avoiding stereotypes.

The lesson will culminate in an exercise in which the children will create their own original and – hopefully – totally believable character. In a subsequent lesson, they can then go on to write a story featuring this character.

Think of characters as real people

The characters who populate our stories are not cardboard cut-outs – at least, they shouldn't be. We should think of them as real people who lead real lives and have real feelings and emotions. Just like us, they are affected by the things that happen to them; events in their life will leave them feeling:

- sad;
- happy;
- angry;
- resentful;
- scared;

- embarrassed;
- and any other powerful emotions that people experience.

We saw this when we were learning about Back Story (Chapter 2) and created a happiness/sadness chart, showing how Cinderella was affected by the major events of her life, so it might be useful to remind the children of it:

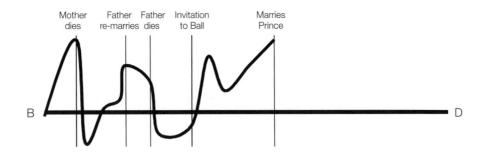

When we are planning all the various incidents that will happen in our stories, we should continually be thinking about how those incidents will affect our characters, in the same way that Cinderella was affected by the things that happened to her. We should be asking ourselves questions like:

- What do our characters think about what happened?
- How are they feeling?
- How will they react to the situation?
- What are they likely to do?

The answers will depend on what type of person they are. Are they:

- Brave or cowardly?
- Reckless or cautious?
- Kind or cruel?
- Optimistic or pessimistic?
- Honest or a bit dodgy?
- Trustworthy or unreliable?

Which of those apply to our characters? Well, that's entirely up to us – as writers, we're the ones in control. Our characters will have the personalities that we give them.

We can have a lot of fun creating characters – for example, we can get them to act out our fantasies for us. *We* might not be good enough at gymnastics to win an Olympic medal at the age of 15, but we can create a character who *is*. We might be limited to kicking a football around in the playground, but our character could score the winning goal at Wembley. We might be shy and a bit timid, but we can create a character who is daring, adventurous, scared of nothing – a character who does things we wouldn't dare do ourselves.

We're going to be creating our own characters in just a moment, but first we should consider something which may not, at first glance, seem all that important – the names we give to our characters. Does it really matter what we call them? Well, actually, it does.

The Importance of names

Names matter, because what a person is called can affect our perception of them. To illustrate the point, try the children with this:

> There are three boys who hang out together, their names are:
>
> ■ Timothy Flowers;
>
> ■ Julian Summerfield;
>
> ■ and Karl Grimes.
>
> Which one is the toughest?

Unless they are wanting to sabotage the lesson, the children will surely opt for Karl Grimes, which begs the question: Why? We don't know anything about these people. All we know are their names.

In my workshops, the most common response I get is usually something along the lines of: 'Well, he just *sounds* hard!' But when I press them further, their reasons for choosing Karl Grimes start to emerge:

Flowers, Summer and Field are all 'nice' words with pleasant connotations; Grimes sounds like crimes.

But there are other reasons – ones that might not be so immediately apparent: for one thing, the single syllables of 'Karl' and 'Grimes' mean that the name is pronounced in a staccato fashion, making the delivery more aggressive than the multi-syllabic, mellifluous Timothy Flowers and Julian

Summerfield. That's not an easy concept for children to get their heads around – but their ears will tell them that longer words often sound gentler than short words, and perhaps we should leave it at that!

Easier for them to grasp is another reason for the name Karl Grimes sounding tougher than the other two: the fact that the initial consonants K and G are quite harsh sounds. Get them to say the letters out loud and see how guttural they sound.

Tolkien used harsh sounds to powerful effect in naming the orcs in *The Lord of the Rings*. How do these sound to the children?:

- Uglúk;
- Muzgash;
- Grishnákh.

Even if you didn't know that orcs were nasty, you wouldn't want to meet those guys after hearing their names!

Charles Dickens was particularly good at matching names to characters. Try asking the children whether they think these people are nice or nasty:

- Uriah Heep;
- Wackford Squeers;
- Tommy Traddles;
- Ned Cheeryble.

The first two are villains, of course, and Tommy and Ned are nice guys – but one thing they all have in common is that they have interesting names. Even if we don't like him, we'd probably want to know more about somebody called Wackford Squeers.

Giving our characters memorable names is one way of making them interesting. Another way is by making them unusual in some way. To achieve this, we should try to avoid the following:

Stereotypes

We're all familiar with stereotypes – we come across them in lots of stories and films:

- stepmothers are wicked;
- orphans are downtrodden;

- villains dress in black …
- … and dogs snarl at them when they enter the room;
- if the villain is intent on world domination, he will often sit stroking a cat as he plots his next act of destruction;
- gangs of children often feature a really clever one, who wears glasses and is often given the nickname Brains;
- the gang may also include a big, tough character who is a bit thick;
- neither of these will be the leader of the gang – that role will go to someone else;
- private investigators are usually men who operate out of run-down, shabby offices;
- uniformed policemen are often fat and bumbling and they never solve crimes because child detectives usually crack the case first.

Ask the children what other examples of stereotypes they can think of – five minutes of fun in the middle of a lesson never hurt anyone!

There are often quite good reasons why these stereotypes have developed over the years. For example:

- If orphans are downtrodden, we feel sorry for them and care about what happens to them, as in Cinderella, and stepmothers can be wicked to them because they're not actually related. If it was a *mother* behaving like that, we'd be appalled!
- If the police solve the crime, the child detectives will have failed, and they are the ones we are rooting for. I'm still not sure why the policemen have to be fat, though …

But although there might be good reasons for certain stereotypes, that's no excuse for repeating them time and time again. Young writers should try to steer clear of them. On the other hand, should they decide to create characters who are the *opposite* of stereotypes, there is a lot of fun to be had. People would surely enjoy reading a story that featured characters like this:

- A sweet-looking little girl who is the best fighter in the gang. She's a Brownie with badges in unarmed combat and First Aid (because her opponents usually need it!).
- A mild-mannered little old lady who decides to try her hand at mugging because she's finding it hard to manage on her pension.

■ A middle-aged teacher whose mother insists on taking him to school every morning because she doesn't like him crossing the road on his own.

Using a bit of imagination and defying stereotypes, we can create characters that will surprise our readers – and our stories will be more interesting as a result.

Creating a character

So, bearing in mind the importance of names and avoiding stereotypes, let's now create our own characters, with the children working together in groups of around three or four. They will be given a photograph of a child and told to imagine that he or she is the Main Character in a story that they will be writing – so they will need to know everything there is to know about that person. They will need to bring that character to life.

For this exercise, you will need two documents supplied in the Teacher resources section at the back of the book:

■ Who Is This Character? – Boy.
■ Who Is This Character? – Girl.

I usually print these double-sided, so that the groups have the choice of creating a male or female character. Laminating the printed sheets is a good idea, since children sometimes absent-mindedly make notes on them, even when asked not to! As mentioned in the Introduction, the documents in the Teacher resources section can be used as a template for creating alternative sheets containing different photos featuring children of a different age or ethnicity, for example, or possibly adults. Each sheet includes a list of questions which prompt the children to think in-depth about their character and really get to know them. If you should decide to create sheets featuring adults, then the questions should be amended accordingly, replacing some of the child-oriented ones with questions such as:

■ What is her job?
■ Is she single/married/divorced/a widow?
■ Does she have children?
■ etc.

As you will see, the questions relevant to child characters are these:

- What is his name?
- How old is he?
- What is his family like?
- What sort of house does he live in?
- What does he do in his spare time?
- What are his likes and dislikes?
- Is he clever?
- Is he popular, with lots of friends?
- What sort of school does he go to?
- Do you like him or dislike him? Why?
- Is he adventurous?
- What would he like to be when he grows up?
- Why would readers identify with him?
- Give me one surprising fact about him.

These are for the children's guidance only, to get them thinking about different aspects of the character's life. They should be warned that they are not necessarily the questions you will ask them when you are quizzing them about the character later in the lesson! However, you *will* be asking them why readers would identify with the character – what they would find interesting or attractive about him or her – and you will be asking about the 'surprising fact', since this could well be a key element in the story that they will eventually write about this character.

When the sheets have been distributed, you should allow the children about 10 minutes to give their character a personality. Is this character good or bad? … Adventurous or shy? … Trustworthy or unreliable? It might help the children if you were to write some character traits on the whiteboard – the 'type of person' list of bullet points on p. 36 might be useful in this respect.

The children may wish to jot down notes about their character, or they may prefer just to talk through their ideas with the other people in their group. Either is fine, just as long as they are able to come up with some answers when you start to grill them about the person in the photograph.

In my workshops, I usually start the interrogation process by asking the children one or two questions from the list provided with the photograph. They are usually comfortable with this – but then the fun starts when, having lulled them into a false sense of security, I put them on the spot by deviating from the list and asking them questions like:

- Could he keep a secret?
- If you were in trouble, would he help you?
- Would you want to go on holiday with him?
- Is he good at sport?
- Does he play an instrument?
- What type of music does he like?
- What is his favourite takeaway?
- Are there any foods that he absolutely hates?
- Does he have a pet?
- Does he have any bad habits?
- What is his favourite TV programme?
- Have the neighbours ever complained about him?

Children can be surprisingly good at coming up with answers, even if they weren't expecting the question. Most of the ones I have worked with seem to enjoy the challenge of thinking on their feet – which is just as well, since the answers they give will immediately be followed by other questions:

- If the character has a pet – what kind? And what is its name? If it's a dog – does your character have to take it for walks? How often? Where does he/she take it?
- If the character has a favourite band – has she ever been to see them? What was the gig like? What's her favourite song of theirs?
- If the neighbours have complained about him – what does he do to annoy them? Does he feel guilty about it? Do his parents believe him or the neighbours?
- etc.

What we are trying to get the children to do here is to envisage their characters having a real life, in which real things happen to them. When quizzing the children in this way, workshop leaders and teachers should watch out for inconsistencies in the things they say about their characters.

For example, in one workshop, a boy told me that his character had seven brothers and sisters – and yet he said that the family car was a Mini. I was intrigued as to how that would work when they all went out together – did they travel in shifts?

Another time I was told that a character lived with his family in a large mansion. And yet, apparently, his mother was a housewife and his father's job was to stack the shelves in a supermarket – which begged the question: 'How can they afford to live in a house like that?'

The children should be questioned in some depth about their character's 'surprising fact'. Teachers and workshop leaders should try to get them to elaborate on this as much as possible – 'How did that come about?' 'Does anybody else know?' 'What exactly happened?' 'How does she feel about it?' 'Wow – tell me more!' – since in talking about it in some detail, the children will often find themselves creating a story.

And that is the next step for them – taking the characters they have created and building a story around them. But before they do, they may want to take on board some final tips which are provided in the next chapter …

CHAPTER

Writing a story

With the character they created in the previous lesson and (hopefully!) a good idea for a plot, developed either from their character's 'surprising fact' or by using one of the methods outlined in Chapter 3, the children should now have all the ingredients for an entertaining and original story.

So how should they set about writing it?

Following the principles of the Obstacles Structure, their thought processes should go something like this:

- How do I make the reader identify with my Main Character?
- What is my character's journey?
- What is the Inciting Incident that sets him/her off on that journey?
- What obstacles does my character have to overcome?
- Can I think of any False Horizon moments to add extra drama?
- What does my character learn from the journey and how does s/he change?
- Do the things s/he learns perhaps help him/her complete the journey?
- Will my character's journey end in success or failure?

But before they put pen to paper, there are still some important things that they need to decide:

- How will my story begin?
- Where will I end it?
- Whose point of view will I write it from?

And that's what we'll be covering in this chapter.

The importance of beginnings and endings

Children are told that stories have a beginning, a middle and an end, and there's no denying it. But a writer doesn't necessarily think of them in that order – I know *I* don't. When I have an idea for a story and am starting to sketch out the plot, I usually follow this sequence:

■   beginning – end – middle;

or occasionally:

■   end – beginning – middle.

Either can work, just as long as the end and the beginning are considered before going on to think about the middle in too much detail – the reason being that a strong opening and a powerful ending are essential elements in a good story. (This is also true of non-fiction writing, as will be shown in Chapter 7.) The opening should grab our attention, draw us into the story and make us want to carry on reading in order to find out what is going to happen; the ending should bring the story to a dramatic and satisfying conclusion.

If we know how we are going to start our story and how the journey is going to end, then the middle will usually take care of itself. We know where our story is going, we know some of the things that are going to happen and so there is going to be a logical progression to what we write. We may change some of the details and incidents along the way, as new and better ideas suggest themselves; we may add new elements to the plot – but if we know the ultimate destination of our story, then it is easier to stay focused and we have a better chance of bringing it to a good, powerful ending.

Where to begin?

As we saw in Chapter 2, being invited to the ball and meeting and falling in love with the Prince – the story of Cinderella as we know it – was just one episode in Cinderella's life:

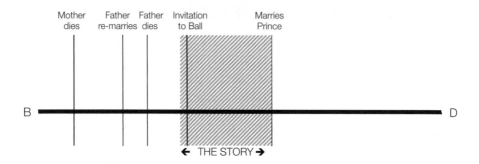

Lots of dramatic things had happened to her before the invitation to the ball – and any one of those could have been the starting point for the story. The writer could have begun it when Cinderella's mother died, when her father re-married or when he died. That would have made the story longer – but would it have been any better? Probably not.

Instead, the writer chose to begin the story *a little before the Inciting Incident*. This meant that the characters and situation could be established before the main action began. At the start of the Disney film, we see Cinderella singing to her friends the animals, who clearly adore her – indicating that she is a really lovely person. We then see her doing all the domestic chores and taking breakfast in bed to her ungrateful stepmother and stepsisters – so we know she is being bullied and exploited. Because of these scenes, we empathise with our Main Character before her journey begins with the invitation to the ball. Putting in a scene or two to set up the character and background before the main plot starts to unfold is not the only way of starting a story, as we will see, but it is a pretty good model for young writers to follow during their early attempts at fiction writing.

A good way to get children thinking about how and where to begin their stories is to read them the first few lines of some well-known books, and to ask their opinion of them. Did they make them want to read on? Did the author 'hook' them?

This is the opening of Nina Bawden's *The Peppermint Pig*:

> Old Granny Greengrass had her finger chopped off in the butcher's when she was buying half a leg of lamb …

Are the children intrigued by this opening? Are they curious to know how on earth Granny Greengrass managed to get her finger chopped off and how she reacted?

Charlotte's Web by E.B. White begins like this:

> 'Where's Papa going with that axe?' said Fern to her mother as they were setting the table for breakfast. 'Out to the hoghouse,' replied Mrs. Arable. 'Some pigs were born last night.'

Are they hooked from the very start? Do they get the feeling that something awful is about to happen, unless Fern can prevent it?

Somewhat different is the opening to Roald Dahl's *Matilda*:

> It's a funny thing about mothers and fathers: even when their own child is the most disgusting little blister that you could ever imagine, they still think that he or she is wonderful. Some parents go further. They become so blinded by adoration they manage to convince themselves their child has qualities of genius. Well, there's nothing very wrong with all this. It's the way of the world. It's only when the parents begin telling us about the brilliance of their own revolting offspring, that we start shouting, 'Bring us a basin! We're going to be sick!'

There is no incident or potential incident here – the action is still to come. But wouldn't the humour and the style make the children want to read on? Wouldn't they feel that there was lots of fun in store?

What do they make of the opening to *Lord of the Flies* by William Golding?:

> The boy with fair hair lowered himself down the last few feet of rock and began to pick his way towards the lagoon. Though he had taken off his school sweater and trailed it now from one hand, his grey shirt stuck to him and his hair was plastered to his forehead. All around him the long scar smashed into the jungle was a bath of heat …

What is a boy in school uniform doing in this tropical environment? What is that long scar smashed into the jungle? There should be plenty to intrigue the children here. It would be a good idea to give them a very brief outline of the plot – something along the lines of 'A party of schoolboys are being evacuated during a war when their plane crashes on a deserted island, and they end up turning into savages' – before going on to discuss the very important point of *where the story begins*.

It doesn't begin with the schoolboys being evacuated, nor with the plane crash itself. Golding cuts straight to the chase: the Inciting Incident – the crash

– has happened, now how will the boys survive? The Back Story can be filled in a little later. It's very dramatic, like the opening of a film – and it aims to hook the reader right from the very start.

If the children are not too young or of a nervous disposition, you could try them with the opening of an adult book by the highly respected Irish author Flann O'Brien – *The Third Policeman*:

> Not everybody knows how I killed old Phillip Mathers, smashing his jaw in with my spade; but first it is better to speak of my friendship with John Divney because it was he who first knocked old Mathers down by giving him a great blow in the neck with a special bicycle pump which he manufactured himself out of a hollow iron bar …

Intriguing, or what? I have known children as young as 10 wanting to get their hands on a copy of the book so that they can read on. I usually suggest that they wait a few years!

The examples given above are a varied bunch; there are all sorts of ways to begin a story. But one thing they all have in common is that they are aiming to engage the reader right from the very start – and that's what the children should aim to do as well. And having given some thought to the opening of their story, they will also need to consider …

Where to end?

The conclusion of the Character Journey seems like a good place to end – after all, that is what the story has been working towards. But it is usually necessary to add a little bit at the end – a postscript to the journey, if you like – in order to make the ending totally satisfactory for our readers. After all, there may still be things that they want to know.

If we look back at the diagram of Cinderella's lifeline shown earlier in this chapter, we will see that after she marries the Prince there is a blank space. That is her future, and since our readers have got to know and like Cinderella during the story, they may well be a little curious about what happens to her next. Has her life changed for the better? This is dealt with very simply in the story, in a single line – 'And they lived happily ever after' – indicating that Cinderella's journey had brought about the desired result.

Lots of other stories have more elaborate endings than that, of course, but at this early stage in their writing careers, it is best if children aim for an ending which is simple and straightforward, but still satisfying for the reader.

So suggest to them that they add a paragraph or short scene after the conclusion of the journey, which addresses any or all of the following questions:

- What has been the effect of the journey on our characters?
- How might it affect them in the future?
- Have they learned things from it – and do we need to show our readers that?
- Are there any loose ends in the story that need to be tied up?

If they do, their story will be all the better for it. And although no doubt they will be itching to get started on it – preferably by writing an *outline* first (see Chapter 2) – there is still one final thing for them to think about:

Point of view

Whose point of view will the children write their stories from? It's something they may not have considered – but they ought to. They will need to decide whether they will write in the first person or the third person.

Writing in the *first person* means that they will be telling the story from the point of view of their Main Character (or possibly one of the other ones): 'I did this ... I told him that ... etc.' Children can often be tempted to write the story in this way, especially if they identify strongly with the Main Character – but they should be aware of the pitfalls:

If you are writing in the first person, you are limiting what you can write about. You can only include things in your story that your narrator sees and experiences personally.

If the story of Cinderella were written from her point of view, it would mean that we could only include incidents that had happened to *her*. We wouldn't be able to include some essential scenes, like the Prince finding the slipper and conducting his search for the person it belonged to. Cinderella would only know about that if someone told her about it at a later date. In the case of the Disney version, we would have to lose some of the scenes featuring the mice – for example, the scene in which they worked in secret to make a dress for Cinderella, or their efforts to get hold of the key so that they could free her from her room.

Hopefully, this will persuade the children that writing in the first person is not something they should attempt at this stage. It *can* be very effective, and lots of great books have been written in this way, but it isn't easy, especially for children.

So steer them in the direction of writing in the *third person*, in which the *writer*, rather than one of the characters, is the narrator of the story: 'He did this … She said that … etc.' If the children write in the third person, they will be able to include incidents featuring any number of characters, and write about what those characters are thinking and feeling, too. Their options will be so much wider – and they should find their stories easier to write.

CHAPTER

6

Rewriting

Once young people have written a story, there is a tendency for them to heave a sigh of relief, congratulate themselves on their accomplishment and then move on to something else. The thought of going back through it, to identify any flaws and see what improvements can be made is often anathema to them – so how can they be persuaded to tackle this important task? It may help to point out something which they may have overlooked.

Every book they read, every film or TV programme they watch, will almost certainly not be a first draft. The writer will have rewritten and polished it – probably several times – until it is as good as he or she can make it.

You may also find it useful to get them thinking about this: if they enjoy playing video games – and which child doesn't? – they are unlikely to be satisfied with the score they achieve at their first attempt. They just *know* they can do better next time – and so they will play the game again and again, watching their high score mount as their expertise grows. So it is with writing – first drafts are a good beginning, but they can always be improved upon.

Nobody is suggesting that children should rewrite and rewrite time and time again, as many professional writers do, but they will find that doing a *second draft* of their story will make it so much better. If they have written the story on a computer, then rewriting is relatively easy – word processing is a boon in that respect; if it has been written in longhand, the task is more time-consuming, but still well worth the effort.

When they have been persuaded that writing a second draft is a good idea, give them some tips on the following.

How to rewrite effectively

It's not really a good idea to start on a second draft immediately after completing the first draft; you should allow yourself time to think about what you have written before making any substantial changes.

So when you have finished writing your story, read it through and correct any spelling mistakes or missing punctuation and then put it to one side. Think about it on and off for a day or two and you may well find yourself having some good ideas for extra little bits that you can add to it: a way of making an incident more exciting; a funny or dramatic line that one of the characters might say; and so on. If you *do* have any ideas like that, make a note of them so you won't forget.

After a couple of days, read your story through again and, as you are reading it, try to imagine that it isn't you who has written it, but someone else – someone who has asked you for your honest opinion of it.

As you read it, ask yourself questions like:

- Does that make sense?
- Is that believable?
- Would that character really do that – or say that?
- Is there a better way of putting that?
- How could the story be improved?

Make a note of anything you think needs to be changed and then ask someone else to read the story – perhaps a friend, a parent or a teacher. Ask them if there is anything you could add or change that would make the story better. And ask them to be *honest*. It may be very flattering for people to tell you that your story is great, but it doesn't help you much. Even if it *is* great, it could always be greater!

Other people's suggestions can be very helpful, as we found when developing story outlines (Chapter 2). When we are writing stories, we get very involved in them; it becomes difficult for us to stand back and consider them objectively. Other people, who aren't as close to the story as we are, can often spot little flaws that we may have overlooked.

Here's an example to try out on the children, taken from an actual story written by a girl who had taken part in one of my workshops, which she had asked me to check through for her.

The plot revolved around Maddy, a young girl who goes to stay in her big sister's flat. Sharing the flat is Maddy's idol – a teenage pop star named Kelsey Sanders, who is hiding out there, on the run from some mysterious villains. Maddy begs to have her photograph taken with Kelsey – a photo which she then uploads to her social networking site. And then this happens, as Kelsey spots the photo while looking at Maddy's profile:

Kelsey looked at it closely. 'OH NO!' She leapt up, pointing at the screen, horrified.

Because, scribbled on a piece of paper in the background, quite visible, was the address where Kelsey Sanders was hiding.

It's a great Inciting Incident – Kelsey's hiding place is no longer a secret and her enemies are likely to turn up on her doorstep at any moment – but what's wrong with it? Does it ring true with the children? It didn't with me, for two reasons:

1. Would anyone *really* be able to read an address scribbled on a piece of paper in the background of a small photo on the internet? I wouldn't have thought so.
2. And why would one of the flat-mates have scribbled their address down anyway?

The change I suggested was very small: add a scene earlier in the story, in which one of the flat-mates receives a parcel from her mother, wrapped in brown paper with the address written on it in black felt-tip pen. It's the sort of thing that would easily get left on a coffee table, and the bold lettering – printed so that it would be easy for the postman to read – would be clearly visible in a photograph.

That's much more believable than the original version; it doesn't leave the reader with that nagging doubt: 'Would that *really* happen?'

By reading the story through carefully and critically yourself and by asking someone else to give you *their* opinion, any flaws like that one can easily be corrected in a second draft – and your story will be all the better for it.

Remember, rewriting is something that *all* writers do – even the very best of them rarely get it right first time!

Non-fiction

CHAPTER

7

Non-fiction writing –
an overview

Non-fiction writing can take many forms: writing to inform, explain, describe, persuade, argue, advise, analyse, review, comment, imagine, explore or entertain. It's quite a list and one which, at first glance, would appear to require a wide variety of different skills.

Fortunately for the teacher or workshop leader, that isn't really the case. The content, approach and style may vary, but many of the basic principles of good and effective structure remain the same whatever type of writing is being tackled. And the children will already be aware of some of those principles if they have been taught how to structure a fiction story.

As we saw in Chapter 5, stories may have a beginning, a middle and an end, but a writer may well think of them in a different order: beginning – end – middle or, alternatively: end – beginning – middle. The reason for this is that *the beginning and ending are of paramount importance* – and that principle holds true whether you are writing fiction or non-fiction.

It doesn't mean that no effort is required in writing the middle section – far from it – but when writers know how they will begin their piece and where it is heading, the part in between becomes so much easier to write. In non-fiction writing, this approach means that the writer can achieve an effective 3-step structure:

1. grab the attention of your readers at the beginning;
2. tell them what you want to impart in a logical sequence that flows naturally, leading up to …
3. an ending that brings your piece to a natural conclusion and leaves your readers informed, entertained and satisfied.

In subsequent chapters we will be looking in detail at some of the more common types of non-fiction writing and showing the children how best to approach them. But before we start to get specific, it would be useful to cover some general points about writing:

- Always bear in mind who you are writing for.
- You can say the same thing in lots of different ways.
- Use all the vocabulary at your disposal.

I have devised exercises/games (they are a bit of both) to illustrate these three points and they have proved to be a popular part of my workshops. Teachers or workshop leaders may choose to use these exercises individually in relevant lessons as a bit of light relief if the children's attention is starting to wander – but it might be worth considering bundling them all together into one lesson, as a general introduction to non-fiction writing.

Bear in mind who you are writing for

Writers should always ask themselves: 'Who will be reading this?' Will it be a child, an adult, a friend, someone in authority, a member of the general public, an expert? Stories, articles, essays, letters – any piece of writing – can be tackled in many different ways, and the style and content of the piece will depend on who you are writing for. To illustrate the point, try putting this scenario to the children:

> It's the first day back at school after the Christmas holidays. The weather has been freezing and when the school staff arrived early in the morning they found that some of the water pipes had burst and the heating system wasn't working. The school will have to be closed and the children sent home.

Because you're such a good writer, the head teacher has asked you to draft a letter to be sent to parents, explaining what has happened. You also have another message to write: your best friend has been away on a family holiday over Christmas and is not due to return until tomorrow, so you want to send him or her a text containing the news that school is closed.

> How would those two messages differ?

It's not really necessary to get the children to write the letter and the text – a class discussion of how they would approach the two tasks will usually suffice.

Depending on their age and level of ability, the children may need a little prompting, but what we want them to recognise is this:

- While the content of the two missives will be fairly similar, the style will be very different: the first one will be a formal letter written to adults; the second one will be an informal text to a child.

- The parents' reaction to the news will be totally different from the friend's reaction. The letter will pose problems for parents, who may have to make emergency childcare arrangements; it will be apologetic and concerned. The text will no doubt be good news for the friend; no apologies, no concern, just the welcome message: 'School's closed – fantastic!'

Of course, writers don't always know who will be reading their work – in which case, they should take a safety-first middle-of-the-road approach: not overly formal and not too jokey. But if they *do* know – or at least have a fairly good idea – then they should bear their readership in mind while writing.

Telling young people that they should always think about who their target audience is can have its down-side: it probably means that every time a teacher sets a piece of work, he or she will be greeted with cries of: 'Sir ... Miss ... who am I writing this for?' But that's a small price to pay for getting pupils into good writing habits!

Different ways of saying the same thing

In non-fiction writing, it's often necessary to say the same sort of thing on more than one occasion, which can easily lead to repetition. In the previous section, for example, I had to write about sending different types of messages, so in order to avoid becoming repetitive, I wrote: ' ... a letter to be sent to parents ... another message to write ... send him or her a text ...'. I even threw in a 'missive' for good measure.

It's not always easy to avoid repeating yourself (there's another example: 'lead to repetition ... becoming repetitive ... repeating yourself' – I managed to say the same thing three times without any ... er ... duplication!), but it's something that children should aim for. And the following exercise should show them that it might not be as difficult as they think.

It's based on the fact that, while all the links between TV programmes sound as if they have been made up on the spot by the station announcer – ('And now there's drama as we join ...') – they have, in fact, usually been scripted by someone. I should know – when I was a Promotion Scriptwriter in television, it used to be part of my job!

The challenge for the children is that they have to write five introductions to the TV soap *Emmerdale* – one for each day of the week – without knowing anything at all about the content of that specific programme (which I often didn't). And all five have to be different.

In my workshops, I usually give the children (working in groups) five minutes to come up with the five different intros and then get them to read out their suggestions. I make a game of it by seating one representative from each group in a chair in the middle of the room, as if they are being interrogated, and putting them under pressure by telling them: 'It's Monday, it's 7 o'clock ...' and giving them a cue. Then, as soon as they have read out their first intro, I leap straight in with 'It's Tuesday, it's 7 o'clock ...' and so on. The sense of urgency adds to the fun; the children enjoy it and they seem to get a sense of achievement and a confidence boost when they successfully negotiate the challenge.

The intros don't have to be *totally* different – that would be too much to ask – just a *bit* different. For example:

- And now on ITV – *Emmerdale*.
- Time now for today's edition of *Emmerdale*.
- Now let's see what's happening in *Emmerdale*.
- There's drama now as we visit *Emmerdale*.
- Now it's time to catch up with *Emmerdale*.

The same thing said in five different ways – no problem. And avoiding repetition is not the only reason for exploring different ways of phrasing something. Quite often, a writer will consider several alternative ways of imparting a piece of information before deciding upon the one which he or she considers to be the best – and the above exercise will give the class valuable practice in doing that.

Using your full vocabulary

How many of us push our vocabulary to the limits? Probably not that many – and young people can be particularly guilty of this: everything is 'brilliant' or 'awesome' or 'wicked' or 'ace' or whatever the current buzz-word happens to be. In my day, back in the Sixties, it was 'fabulous' or 'groovy' ... but let's not go there.

Children know a lot more words than they think they do – and the proof is to be found in the following exercise, for which you will need three documents from the Teacher resources section at the back of the book:

- Green Day Rock the Leeds Festival;
- Awesome;
- Brilliant.

You will also need a small bag of some kind – an ordinary carrier bag will do.

You will need to print just one copy each of Awesome and Brilliant and then cut out 11 individual slips of paper – five of one word and six of the other – which you should then fold up and place in the bag. The children will be taking them out one by one, as though drawing a raffle. Incidentally, if 'awesome' and 'brilliant' have been superseded in the buzz-word stakes by the time you read this, please feel free to substitute any suitable words of your choice!

Print up as many copies of Green Day Rock the Leeds Festival as you need (as you will see, each A4 page contains two copies of the document) and distribute them to the children, keeping one for yourself, to make notes on.

GREEN DAY ROCK THE LEEDS FESTIVAL

_____ guitar playing by Billie Joe Armstrong, and _____ drumming from Tre Cool sent the crowd wild as Green Day's _____ musicianship stole the show at the Leeds Festival. The atmosphere was _____ as the _____ threesome put together the most _____ set imaginable, starting with their _____ new single 'American Idiot' and winding up with Queen's _____ 'We Are the Champions'. The performance was _____ from start to finish. _____ gig. _____ band!

This document is inspired by a review that I saw on the internet, after the band Green Day had appeared at an open-air gig. The review contained a great deal of repetition, in which the same adjectives were used time and time again – it was truly awful, but it gave me the idea for this exercise. And this is how it works …

Start by telling the children how easy it is to get lazy in our use of words; we tend to use the same words over and over again, without trying to think of alternatives. You want to show them what can happen if we aren't careful in our selection of words, so you have taken a review of Green Day at the Leeds Festival and removed a number of words which are all of the same kind. Hopefully they should realise that all the blanks represent adjectives – if not, a bit of prompting might be in order.

Tell them that the bag contains a selection of adjectives, which will be chosen at random and used to fill in the blanks. How good will the finished review be if we don't put any thought into our choice of words? Let's find out ...

As the children take turns in drawing adjectives from the bag and calling them out, it shouldn't take long for them to realise that something odd is happening. When the second 'awesome' or 'brilliant' comes out, they will probably think it is a mistake; when the third one comes out, they will know they have been tricked.

Fill in the blanks on your copy of the document as the adjectives are called out, and then read the finished review. It will sound ridiculous – but point out to the children that it is not a *total* exaggeration. How many times have *they* repeated a word *ad nauseam*?

Depending on how the adjectives come out, the children may notice something interesting: if the same word is drawn out to fill the last two blanks, so that it reads 'Awesome gig. Awesome band!' (or 'brilliant' for both, of course), it actually sounds pretty good. Repetition *can* be used for dramatic effect, but we won't go into that here!

Instead, let's see if the class can come up with some adjectives of their own – and definitely *not* 'awesome' or 'brilliant' – that could be used to fill the gaps. Challenge them to reach a specific target – say 25 – and then get them to call out their suggestions, which you should write on the whiteboard. I have found that children seriously underestimate the number of words they know; often they will think that coming up with 25 suitable adjectives is totally beyond them, only to find the list on the whiteboard going past 30 ... 35 ... 40 and more.

And finally, let's end this chapter with ...

Some golden rules for writing non-fiction

Be clear in your mind about what you want to say. If you aren't absolutely certain what it is that you're trying to tell your readers, then you are unlikely to be able to put your message across effectively. Learning how to identify the Key Point, which is something that we will be covering in the next chapter, will prove very useful in this respect.

When you know what you want to say – say it clearly. Imagine that you are face-to-face with your readers, passing on information to them in a way that they will easily understand. Try to use short, snappy sentences. When readers are confronted with long, rambling sentences with lots of sub-clauses, their attention can easily start to wander; the point that the writer is trying to get across can easily be lost; the impact of the writing is diluted. Yet sometimes, a long sentence is necessary when you want to make a series of points that are linked (as in my previous sentence). You may also wish to use a long sentence in order to avoid your writing becoming staccato, with too many short sentences following on from each other. So do what I did in that example above – *break long sentences up with semi-colons*. The semi-colon is a much-neglected tool of grammar, and if children are taught to use it correctly, they will find it extremely useful. There is another benefit, too: since so few people use semi-colons in their writing, they are usually very impressed by writers who *do* use them.

Don't be afraid to start a sentence with a conjunction. Grammatical purists may say that you shouldn't start a sentence with 'And' or 'But' or 'Yet', etc. – but nowadays it is a perfectly acceptable thing to do. And starting with a conjunction is an excellent way of adding punch and power to a sentence – especially a short one.

Hopefully, the general guidelines given in this chapter will be useful to teachers and workshop leaders in lessons covering many different forms of non-fiction writing. The requirements of the curriculum and literacy strategies are always liable to change, as teachers know only too well! But the principles of good and effective writing are universal and they can be used as the basis for teaching to the curriculum – whatever it might be.

8

Writing to inform/journalism

In this lesson we'll be focusing on the art of writing to inform, using journalism as the vehicle, since newspapers and magazines are things that young people are very familiar with, and teachers can provide a wide variety of examples of effective beginnings and endings simply by bringing a couple of newspapers into the lesson.

The children will learn:

■ How to identify the Key Point of what they are writing about.

■ Two effective ways to start a piece of writing.

■ Five effective ways to end it.

They will be writing the opening and closing paragraphs of a newspaper story, with the middle filled in merely as bullet points. However, if the children you are teaching are older or particularly able, you may wish to incorporate into the lesson some tips on how to make the middle part of a story flow in a logical way (see Chapter 15) and ask them to write the story in full.

For this lesson, you will need a whiteboard, smart-board or flip chart on which to list the various ways of starting and ending a story, plus printed examples of news stories, which are provided in the Teacher resources section at the back of the book:

■ What type of intro and ending?

It would also be useful to have some newspapers in the classroom for you and the children to look through in search of further examples. In addition, you will need to print another document from the Teacher resources section:

■ Jacob Brown facts.

The Key Point

The first step in planning a piece of writing is to identify the Key Point. In other words, what is the *essence* of the piece? What is it actually *about*? If someone asked you to sum it up in just a few words, how would you describe it?

The easiest – and most fun – way of getting young people to focus on the Key Point is to tell them about *pitching*. If a writer or producer has an idea for a film and wants to persuade a movie company to make it, they will need to pitch the idea to them – give them a tantalising outline of the story that will convince them they have to reach into their wallets and finance the project.

The most extreme form of pitching is something called the Elevator Pitch. Why is it called that? Well, imagine you were a writer with an idea, and you found yourself sharing a lift with a powerful movie mogul. You would have the opportunity to sell your idea to him, but you'd have to do it in a very short space of time, before the lift stopped and he got out. It would be no use rambling on and saying something like: 'Well, you see, there's this man from Birmingham who's really good at copying people's handwriting. And he's on holiday in Spain when he runs into this shady-looking character in a bar …' DING! The lift stops at the third floor, the movie mogul gets out and your chance has gone.

The Elevator Pitch is short, sharp and to the point – so short, in fact, that it has another name: *pitching in 25 words or less*. (I know that, to be grammatically correct, we ought to use the word 'fewer' rather than 'less' – but try telling that to a media mogul!) Students are often highly dubious that an entire film can be pitched so briefly, but in fact most Hollywood movies can be summed up in under 25 words. For example, the pitch for Ridley Scott's film *Gladiator* was reportedly: 'When a Roman general is betrayed and his family murdered by a corrupt prince, he comes to Rome as a gladiator to seek revenge.'

Get the students to try pitching their favourite movie to you in 25 words or less, and see how they get on; it will focus their mind wonderfully on what the key elements are. And after they have struggled, you can stun them with the story of how another Ridley Scott movie idea was said to have been successfully pitched to Hollywood in just three words. The film was the science fiction classic *Alien* and the pitch was a model of economy: '*Jaws* in space.'

If an entire film can be pitched in 25 words or less, then it should be possible to sum up something much shorter – a piece of non-fiction writing such as a newspaper or magazine story – in 15 words or less. Here, in exactly 15 words, is the brief outline for a fictitious news story that we'll be using to illustrate how to begin and end a piece of writing:

'A 10-year-old girl has become the youngest person ever to swim the Channel.'

There will be lots of other information in the piece – full details, background, reactions, etc. – but that's the essence of the story we'll be telling; that's the Key Point. And once it has been identified, we can start to plan how to begin and end our story.

Two ways to start a piece of writing

Generally speaking, the opening (or intro) to a newspaper report will fall into one of two categories:

1. The Key Point Opening.
2. The Tease Opening.

As its name suggests, the *Key Point Opening* is a statement of the main message right at the start of the piece. In the case of our story about the young Channel swimmer, that would mean beginning the piece something like this:

> 'At the age of just 10 years and 3 months, Brighton schoolgirl Hayley Wyngarde has become the youngest person ever to swim the Channel.'

This is a straightforward and effective type of opening which you will see in all kinds of newspapers, but which is especially favoured by the broadsheets. If you were writing the story for a tabloid, you might choose to tackle it in a more informal fashion by using a *Tease Opening*. (NB In journalistic circles, this is usually referred to as a 'Delayed Drop', but I have found that calling it a Tease Opening helps children understand the principle more easily.) This type of opening entails teasing your readers by not telling them what the story is about straight away, but leading up to the Key Point in an intriguing way. For example:

> 'Brighton schoolgirl Hayley Wyngarde meets up with her friends every weekend to go swimming at the local leisure centre.
>
> But last Saturday, she was unable to join them; Hayley had an important swimming engagement elsewhere – in the English Channel.
>
> And by Sunday morning she had become the youngest person ever to swim from Dover to Calais – at the age of just 10 years and 3 months.'

Using this type of opening, you draw your readers into the story before telling them the crucial facts – and as a result the piece has a lighter feel. A Tease Opening makes it more of a human-interest story than a straightforward news report and is particularly useful when writing feature articles or reviews.

But a word of warning – when using the Tease Opening it is essential not to delay the Key Point for too long, otherwise the readers may find themselves wondering what the story is actually about!

So which opening should the young writer choose? Key Point or Tease? That will depend on the story: as a general rule (and only *very* general), a story dealing with serious issues such as death or destruction would probably be best served by a Key Point opening, while for a more light-hearted story, a Tease opening might be best. Something else to bear in mind when deciding upon an opening is the question we told the children to ask themselves in Chapter 7: 'Who will be reading this?' In the case of the two different messages about school closure which we asked them to think about, the letter to parents – formal in style, giving bad news to adults – would probably have a Key Point opening: 'I'm sorry to have to tell you that school will be closed today'; but the text – informal, giving good news to a friend – might well have a Tease Opening: 'You're going to love this! Best news ever! School is closed!'

Five ways to end

When writing a non-fiction piece, you are not simply presenting a sequence of facts to your readers, you are telling them a story – and a story needs a strong ending. Five effective ways to bring your piece to a satisfying conclusion are:

1. End on a quote.
2. Remind your readers of the Key Point/sum up.
3. Add a final piece of information.
4. Hint at further developments in the story.
5. The Circular Ending – referring back to your opening.

You can use these singly or combine them in different ways: you can use a quote which adds a final piece of information or hints at further developments; the Circular Ending may be a reminder of the Key Point.

So let's see how we might end the channel swimmer story in different ways. If we decided to *end on a quote*, the final paragraph might be:

Hayley said: 'Two miles out from Calais I was feeling so tired that I was tempted to give up. But I kept on going – and now I'm really glad I did. Beating the world record is something I've always dreamed of.'

If we wanted to *remind our readers of the Key Point/sum up*, we could end the piece in this way, which also incorporates a quote:

A spokesman for the Distance Swimming Association said: 'Swimming the Channel is an enormous challenge, even for the most experienced swimmer. To achieve it at the age of 10 is a remarkable feat.'

An ending which *adds a final piece of information* might be:

Hayley beat the record set by French boy Lucien Rius, who was 10 years and 11 months old when he swam the Channel in 1997.

If we wanted to *hint at further developments*, we might end the story in this way:

When she's had time to recover, Hayley will begin training for her next challenge – she's planning to swim the 36km length of Loch Ness later this year.

The *Circular Ending* isn't easy to pull off, but it's extremely effective if you can do it. It entails linking the ending to the intro, as though completing a circle and bringing the story to a deeply satisfying conclusion. A good example is to be found in Chapter 3 of this book: the chapter begins with the scenario of children complaining: 'I don't know what to write about!' – and the same quote is used at the end, to indicate that the problem has hopefully been solved.

The Circular Ending tends to be found more in feature writing than in straightforward news reporting, since it is a stylistic device, but to see how it might be used in our Channel-swimming story, let's assume we had begun with the Tease Opening given above:

Brighton schoolgirl Hayley Wyngarde meets up with her friends every weekend to go swimming at the local leisure centre.

But last Saturday, she was unable to join them; Hayley had an important swimming engagement elsewhere – in the English Channel.

To give the story a Circular Ending, our final paragraph might be:

Hayley is determined to join her friends at the leisure centre next weekend as usual, because the staff there have laid on a special treat for her – a party to celebrate her world record.

And it's not just circular; it hints at further developments, too – a double whammy!

All of the intros and endings to the Channel Swimmer story are listed in a document which you will find in the Teacher resources section at the end of the book, in case you wish to provide the class with hard copies.

Having told the children about the different types of intros and endings, it might be a good idea to see if the information has sunk in by challenging them to try and identify which ones have been used in actual newspaper and magazine stories.

The document *What Type of Intro and Ending?* in the Teacher resources section contains six different stories featuring a variety of openings and endings. These stories are all from a school magazine, so they are fairly child-friendly. The document is designed to be printed double-sided, and it would also be beneficial to laminate it before distributing copies to the class.

The six stories are numbered and the answers to the question *What Type of Intro and Ending?* are:

1. This has a Tease Opening – the Key Point comes in paragraph two; the ending adds a final piece of information about the book.

2. This has a Key Point Opening and ends with a quote – easy peasy!

3. Another Key Point Opening here; the ending hints at further developments – the national finals.

4. This story has a Tease Opening and ends on a quote.

5. This has a Tease Opening – but note that a little bit of key information (the fact that it is an Aim Higher initiative) is mentioned in the opening sentence, despite the fact that the Key Point itself is to be found in paragraph two; the ending combines a quote with a hint of further developments – the students going on to study languages.

6. This has a Tease Opening, with the Key Point given in the second sentence; the ending adds a final piece of information about other twilight classes.

Additionally, you may also choose to give the class a pile of newspapers and challenge them to find good examples of the different types of intros and endings for themselves.

Putting together a news story

Now that the children have learned the theory of how to plan and structure a news story, we can give them some hands-on experience of putting it into practice. To do this, we will use the document entitled *Jacob Brown facts* provided in the Teacher resources section at the end of the book, which hopefully you will have printed out. These are the facts which I gathered during an interview with Jacob Brown – a student at a school where I was working – in order to write a story for the school magazine and the local newspapers.

The challenge for the children is to take these and assemble them into an entertaining and informative story. We will be asking them to:

1. Write the opening of the story, up to and including the Key Point.
2. Give an indication of how the story will continue, by putting the facts in a suitable order.
3. Write the final paragraph of the story.

NB As mentioned earlier, older or more able children who have been taught techniques for filling in the middle may write the story in full.

They can either work individually or in teams of two or three; in my workshops I tend to let KS3 children work in teams and encourage older students to fly solo.

JACOB BROWN FACTS

1. Jacob Brown is 18 and comes from Leeds. He is a 6th former at Allerton Grange School.
2. Jacob belongs to Leeds City Athletics Club and competes in the triple jump and long jump.
3. He used to play basketball, but took up athletics three years ago.
4. Last weekend he won a triple jump gold medal and a long jump bronze medal at the North of England Championships held in Sheffield.
5. When he competed in the triple jump last year, he didn't qualify for the final.
6. His winning distance in the triple jump was 14.50m (his personal best is 15.20m) and in the long jump he achieved 6.46m (personal best 7.46m).
7. On Tuesday, Jacob was asked to bring his medals to the Allerton Grange 6th Form Assembly, where his triple jump winning distance was marked out in string and his schoolmates congratulated him.
8. When Jacob was interviewed, he said: 'Even though I won, I didn't jump as well as I could. But it's early in the season and I'm hoping to get better.'

9. Jacob's ambition is to become the national champion and then to qualify for the Commonwealth Games. The Commonwealth Games trials are in June this year and the qualifying distance is 16m.

10. Jacob said: 'I think I can get it right in time, and if I do, representing my country at the Commonwealth Games would be a great experience. I'd give it my best shot, and hopefully my best might be worth a medal.'

Armed with the list of facts, the class should spend some time in discussing the various options before putting anything down on paper.

The first task is to identify the *Key Point*. What is the story about? What achievement or event makes it newsworthy? There are two events mentioned: Jacob winning two medals at the North of England Championships and the special school assembly. But although the assembly is the more recent event – and newspapers like their stories to appear as up to date as possible (hence all the references in news stories to 'yesterday' and 'last night') – the more important event is the winning of the medals, so that is the Key Point.

Having identified the Key Point, the children must *decide how to begin*. Will they mention the Key Point right at the beginning, or will they lead up to it in a Tease Opening? Facts 3 and 5 could be useful for that – can the class suggest how that might work? If they can't, give them these examples:

> Three years ago, Leeds teenager Jacob Brown had a decision to make: should he carry on playing basketball, or should he switch to athletics? He chose athletics – and now he's delighted that he did. Because last weekend, at the North of England Championships …

> Just 12 months ago, Leeds triple-jumper Jacob Brown was bitterly disappointed when he failed to reach the final in the North of England Championships. But what a difference a year can make …

And *how will they end*? With one of the quotes? By finding a way to re-state the Key Point? By adding a further piece of information – for example, the statistics in fact 6; or facts 3 or 5, if they haven't been used in the opening? By hinting at further developments – maybe fact 9? Can they find a way of achieving a Circular Ending?

With the intro and ending decided upon, we can now think about how to fill in *the middle* – putting the facts that haven't been used in the intro or ending into a logical order that tells the story in a natural and informative way. The children may find that they don't need *all* the facts provided, but they will certainly need most of them.

Whether the children go on to write their stories in the lesson or as a homework assignment is, of course, up to the teacher. But I would highly recommend that the class spend some time afterwards reading out and analysing some of their efforts; these class discussions can be very productive and can lead to some really lively debates about the relative merits of the different approaches.

They also serve to highlight the fact that *all* the different types of intros and endings can be effective – there are more ways than one to write a story.

We will be returning to the Jacob Brown story in Chapter 15, and looking at the full press release that I wrote, and which is included in the Teacher resources section. You may find it useful to have a sneak preview of it now, so that you can see which type of intro and ending I chose to use.

A tsunami news story

If you wish to give the class further practice in writing a news story, there are two documents in the Teacher resources section at the end of the book which you can use:

- South Asian Tsunami Fact-Sheet.
- Beginning And Ending – Tsunami story.

The fact-sheet is primarily intended for use in the persuasive writing lesson contained in the next chapter, but used in conjunction with the Beginning And Ending document it will serve as the basis for an additional exercise in writing to inform. See Chapter 9 for more details.

Persuasive writing I – the poster

What I will be aiming to do in the next two chapters is not to suggest a whole new way of teaching persuasive writing – although some of the approaches may possibly seem novel – but rather to show how professional writing techniques can be used to *augment* the very good work which is already being done in many schools, adding elements and structures that will hopefully give the children's writing more impact.

In this lesson we will only touch briefly on structure; the main focus will be on teaching the children how to *persuade*, by setting them a relatively simple task – writing a poster. I have found this to be good preparation for the more demanding task of writing a persuasive essay – which they will tackle in the next lesson – since the key elements and thought processes involved are pretty much the same, but creating a poster is easier, more fun and is particularly suitable for younger or less able children.

The poster the children will be creating will take the form of an appeal for donations following a natural disaster in the developing world. When I first introduced this persuasive writing module into my workshops several years ago, the most recent high-profile disaster was the South Asian Tsunami of 2004 – and that was the one which I used as the subject of the module. Consequently, that is the disaster which this lesson focuses on, and for which photocopiable worksheets are supplied in the Teacher resources section at the back of the book. The fact that it is still counted as one of the most devastating natural disasters in history makes it as relevant today as it was at the time. However, teachers may wish to use a different disaster on which to base the lesson, in which case they will find it very easy to adapt – although they will, of course, need to produce a different fact-sheet from the one supplied. Perhaps this could be a research project for the class.

For this lesson, some preparation will be needed on the part of the teacher or workshop leader. The worksheets you will need from the Teacher resources section are:

- South Asian Tsunami Fact-Sheet.
- The Tsunami Child.
- Indonesian and Sri Lankan names.

In addition, teachers should *source six or so photographs* of the disaster, preferably featuring children who have suffered as a result of the tsunami. These photographs should be printed (four to a sheet of A4 produces a good size) so that the children can cut them out and stick them on their posters.

When sourcing photographs, try to include some close-up images of children's faces, which look particularly striking in posters. And if the children are looking into the camera, so much the better – eye contact is an extremely effective way of arousing sympathy, which is what the posters will be aiming to do.

The children will need:

- sheets of A3 paper;
- felt-tip pens;
- scissors;
- glue.

Before we get them to think about the content of their posters, we need to teach them something about the art of persuasion, which can be summed up like this:

Get people to see things the same way that *you* do.

And to introduce that idea, begin by reading them a short piece of fiction. It's taken from Alan Bennett's book *Untold Stories* – an extract from the author's diary in which he noted down an idea he'd had for the opening scene of a film.

But a quick note before you read it to the children: the film idea features King Charles I – but do the class know anything about him? If they have studied the Stuart period, all well and good; if they haven't, it might be useful to give them a very brief outline along the lines of: 'Charles I was king of England in the seventeenth century. He wanted to rule without any interference from

Parliament, they objected and eventually this led to a civil war between the King and his supporters and those who supported Parliament. The King's army lost the war, he was put on trial for treason, found guilty and sentenced to be beheaded.' Or something like that!

Now read on. Ask the children to close their eyes and really *listen* as you read the film idea – can they see in their mind's eye what Alan Bennett was seeing in *his*?

> A film beginning with a man being shepherded through a darkened hall; glimpses of paintings, a shaft of light on a plaster ceiling, the gleam of armour but so dark (lines of light around the shutters) that it's hard to see anyone's face. A distant murmur of sound. Odd muttered directions. 'Steady … a step here.' The man steered round sheeted furniture and up uncarpeted stairs. Then the group comes to a stop. Someone knocks on the shutter and it is thrown open, light floods in, there is the sudden roar of the crowd. Charles I steps out onto the scaffold.

Ask the class what was going on in their heads while you were reading. What did they see? The glimpses of paintings … the shaft of light … the gleam of armour … light flooding in as the shutter was opened? And what did they hear? The murmur of sound … the muttered directions … the roar of the crowd? Did they possibly hear the sound of footsteps? They weren't mentioned – but we *were* told that the stairs were uncarpeted.

Alan Bennett had obviously thought through every detail of that scene until he could see the action unfolding in his mind's eye. When he wrote it down, he was trying to make his readers see what *he* was seeing … trying to get them to *visualise* the scene, just as *he* had. He was appealing to his readers' imagination.

How adverts appeal to our imagination

Most advertising is about getting people to imagine things – and that's a form of persuasive writing we're all familiar with. Think of the adverts on TV – what are they saying to the people who are watching them? Essentially, they're saying 'Imagine yourself …':

- playing with this toy;
- eating this food;
- visiting this theme park;
- driving this car;

■ having hair as beautiful as this.

Ask the children to give you some other examples from adverts they have seen, and you will probably be bombarded with suggestions. Adverts are part of the fabric of their lives, which is what makes them such a useful starting point when teaching persuasive writing. In various ways, they try to persuade us that something is good, something is right, we must have it, we must do it. Lots of adverts appeal to people's:

■ greed – I must have that;
■ aspirations – I'd love to look like that.

But what about other kinds of adverts – ones that aren't trying to sell us a product? Adverts for charities, like the NSPCC or the RSPCA? Or appeals following a disaster somewhere in the world? What do the children think *those* kind of adverts are appealing to? It's certainly not our greed or our aspirations. No, adverts like that appeal to:

■ our sympathy;
■ our desire to help those in need;
■ our better nature.

And instead of trying to get us to imagine ourselves owning that fabulous toy or playing that must-have game, they are trying to make us imagine the plight of a neglected child, a mistreated animal or a starving and homeless family. And that's the sort of thing we want the children to do now, as they create a poster about the Asian Tsunami of 2004.

Preparing to make the poster

As with previous exercises, the children can work individually or in small groups – although I find groups preferable. Begin by distributing a copy of the document 'South Asian Tsunami Fact-Sheet' to each group; read it out loud to them and ask them how it makes them feel. Can they imagine what it must have been like to be caught up in a disaster like that?

SOUTH ASIAN TSUNAMI FACT-SHEET

- A tsunami is a series of giant waves.

- Tsunamis are often caused by earthquakes or the eruption of volcanoes.

- The South Asian Tsunami struck on 26 December 2004.

- It was caused by an underground earthquake in the Indian Ocean.

- The earthquake which triggered the tsunami registered between 9.1 and 9.3 on the Moment Magnitude Scale.

- It was the second largest earthquake ever recorded.

- The waves of the tsunami were up to 25 metres high.

- The tsunami devastated many countries on the coast of Asia and Africa.

- Indonesia, Sri Lanka, India and Thailand suffered the worst damage.

- Malaysia, the Maldives, the Seychelles, Kenya, Somalia and Tanzania were also affected.

- Almost 300,000 people were killed and many more were injured.

- 242,000 died in Indonesia, 31,000 in Sri Lanka and 16,000 in India.

- It was one of the worst natural disasters of all time.

- As the waves hit, families were separated from each other, with parents unable to hold on to their children.

- Throughout the region, children were left searching for their parents.

- Many children were orphaned.

- Thousands of families were left homeless and lost their livelihoods.

- Schools were destroyed, making a return to some sort of normal life more difficult for the children.

For this exercise, we're going to imagine that it's a month after the tsunami and money is desperately needed to help the injured, provide medical supplies, rebuild homes and schools and so on. We're going to make a poster that will persuade people to send money. Our aim will be to try to make them *visualise* all the suffering and appeal to their sympathy and their desire to help.

We could do this by telling them what happened in the tsunami and giving them some details of the devastation it caused. But a more effective, more *persuasive*, way might be to focus on the suffering of one child who was a victim of the tsunami – a child who lost his parents, his friends, his home.

Why would it be more effective? Because *it's easier for people to imagine the suffering of one child than the suffering of thousands*. It makes the story more personal, focuses our readers' attention – and once we've done that and got them using their imagination, then we can go on to tell them that this child was one of many thousands who suffered in the tsunami, which is why so much money is needed.

Structuring the message – beginning, middle and end

The children should be aware by now – it has been said often enough! – that the beginning and ending of a piece of writing are very important. So how does that apply here?

Well, in the case of a poster, we could say that the *beginning* is the headline – the message that goes across the top – and probably the first paragraph as well. These are what will draw people to the poster and make them read it. The *ending* is the final statement which will hopefully persuade people to send money. In between those two is the *middle* section in which we provide most of the information.

The headline has got to be something that will grab people's attention, and to help us do that, we're going to include a picture. Illustrations are more eye-catching than text alone, as all advertisers know.

So show the class the *photographs you sourced of children who suffered from the tsunami* and get each group to choose one that they would like to feature in their poster. If they worked for a charity and were doing this for real, they would have all the details of that child – but since they don't, and since this is just an exercise, they are going to make up the details.

They must use their imagination to create a fictitious personal history for that child: name, age, family, background and – most importantly – how he or she was affected by the tsunami. This is very similar to the exercise in Chapter 4, in which the children used a photograph to help them create a fictitious character, so if they have tackled that task previously, they will know what is expected of them here. As in that earlier exercise, it will be useful to provide the pupils with a list of questions to ask themselves about their character – and these are provided in the document entitled 'The Tsunami Child', which can be found in the Teacher resources section of the book. You may prefer to print this up and distribute a copy to each group, so that the children can refer to it while thinking about the character they are creating.

THE TSUNAMI CHILD

SOME QUESTIONS TO ASK YOURSELF

● What is his/her name?

● How old is he/she?

- What did he/she lose?
  - Mother?
  - Father?
  - Both parents?
  - Brothers/sisters?
  - Home?
  - School?
- What happened to him/her *during* the tsunami?
- Was he/she injured?
- What happened to him/her *after* the tsunami?
- How can donations of money help him/her?
  - Rebuild the family home?
  - Rebuild the town or village?
  - Support an orphanage?
  - Rebuild a school?
  - Provide food?

Since most of the children who suffered in the tsunami were Indonesian or Sri Lankan, it will be useful to give each group a copy of the document 'Indonesian and Sri Lankan Names' to add a touch of authenticity to their character. Alternatively, since many of the victims of the tsunami were Islamic, the children may wish to choose Muslim names.

Allow the pupils about 10–15 minutes to create a personal history for the child they have chosen – and also ask them to think about a headline for the poster. If you feel they may need a bit of guidance, here are some examples of headlines which might be effective:

> Don't Abandon Dian;
> Wipe The Tears From Roshan's Eyes;
> A Life In Ruins.

The headline doesn't necessarily have to be a single line. Two lines can be highly effective, especially when they consist of a set-up and pay-off, like this:

> No Parents, No Home, No Future.
> What are you going to do about it?

As with previous exercises, a class discussion of some of the efforts can be useful in helping to refine and shape the initial idea, before the children go on to produce their poster.

Having chosen a photograph and decided on a headline, they now have a *beginning*; the information given in the tsunami fact-sheet, coupled with the character history they have created, should provide them with plenty of material for the *middle*; and a final message urging people to donate money to the Tsunami Appeal will be a suitable *end*.

And so they are ready to start …

An extra challenge

If the class is particularly able, you may wish to make this exercise more challenging by getting them to do *two different versions* of the poster, with half the class producing a poster aimed at adults and the other half doing one aimed at schoolchildren. As we saw in Chapter 7, bearing in mind who you are writing for is very important – and this is a good way of reinforcing that message. The two categories of poster would carry roughly the same message, but they would deliver it in slightly different ways.

We are trying to get our audience to use their imagination and empathise with the victims of the tsunami, and we are using the story of a child to do that. So the underlying message of the poster aimed at schoolchildren might be:

■ Imagine if this had happened to you.

We want the children who see the poster to imagine how horrifying it must be to see your parents being swept away in a flood and your home destroyed: Who will look after you? Where will you live?

The poster for adults would be giving a subtly different message:

■ Imagine if this was your child.

We would want to appeal to the protective instincts that parents have for their families. If you were killed and your children were left as orphans, wouldn't you want someone to care for them?

In both cases, we would be playing on people's emotions – but that is a very effective way of persuading them!

Using the tsunami information in a different way

The document 'South Asian Tsunami Fact-Sheet' can also be used to give pupils more practice in writing to inform. In Chapter 8, we presented them with information about the triple-jumper Jacob Brown and asked them to write the beginning and ending of a press story. If you wish, you could get them to do the same with the tsunami information.

They would be writing the intro and ending to a *news story* about the tsunami, not a story about an individual child, as they did in their persuasive writing. They would need to consider which of the two different types of intro would be more effective, and also which of the five endings to opt for, with the middle section filled in as bullet points.

Depending on their ability, you may wish to let them tackle the task with no further guidance from you, other than a reminder of the types of beginnings and endings, or you could give them some examples before they begin. If you decide on the latter, you will find the document 'Beginning and Ending – Tsunami Story' useful.

TWO WAYS TO BEGIN:

Key Point Opening:

A massive tsunami swept across the Indian Ocean today, devastating coastal areas and causing thousands of deaths.

Tease Opening:

It was just another Sunday in the Indonesian city of Banda Aceh: people going about their business, children playing on the seafront, fishing boats bobbing in the harbour.

But in less than a minute, people, boats and buildings were all swept away by an 18-metre wall of water as the tsunami struck.

FIVE WAYS TO END:

Reminding readers of the Key Point:

With thousands of people dead and communities destroyed in many countries around the Indian Ocean, the tsunami was one of the worst natural disasters of all time.

Adding a final piece of information:

The earthquake which triggered the tsunami registered between 9.1 and 9.3 on the Moment Magnitude Scale, making it the second largest earthquake ever recorded.

Hinting at further developments:

As the scale of the devastation became clear, governments around the world promised help for the stricken region. A 150-strong UK medical team will be flying out to Indonesia today, with more aid teams to follow in the next few days.

The Circular Ending:

It began just like any other Sunday – but as evening fell, the people of Banda Aceh who were lucky enough to survive knew that they had witnessed a day that none of them would ever forget.

Ending on a quote:

The utter devastation wrought by the tsunami was summed up by one local, when he said: 'There used to be streets here – now there's nothing but rubble and mud. I saw a wrecked car wedged in the branches of a tree and a fishing boat dumped on the roof of a house. It was just like a nightmare.'

As you will see, some of the material used in these openings and endings is not to be found in the fact-sheet. The information about Banda Aceh was culled from the internet, so if you want to give the class some background about what happened there, you will find there is plenty available; perhaps they could research the story. As for the quote – I made it up, based on what had happened in Banda Aceh. If the children wish to use a quote ending, they will need to do the same; it will be good practice for them in creative writing!

10

Persuasive writing II – the essay

Having introduced the children to some basic principles of persuasion in the previous lesson, we are now going to set them a more demanding task – writing a persuasive essay.

In my experience, the most predominant method of teaching children how to write one of these seems to be suggesting that they follow a template which goes something like this:

1. State the issue you are addressing and say what your position is.

2. Argue your case.

3. End with a summary of your position.

Let's look at that in terms of the different types of beginnings and endings which were described in Chapter 8.

Supposing the essay was about the dangers of smoking – an extremely popular topic in persuasive writing – then we would probably say that something along the lines of 'I believe that smoking is very dangerous/unpleasant/anti-social/etc.' was the Key Point. So a piece of writing based on the above template would have a Key Point opening and an ending which reminds readers of the Key Point/sums up.

It would work structurally and it would serve to get the message across – but, as we have seen, there are at least two different ways to begin a piece of non-fiction writing effectively and five or more different ways to end. So there are alternatives to the standard template – alternatives which may well produce writing that is not only more persuasive, but also more enjoyable to read. I would recommend that pupils be encouraged to consider the various options available to them rather than sticking rigidly to the standard template.

In my workshops, the subject I ask pupils to write about is:

Should Overseas Aid be cut?

It follows on neatly from the poster exercise, with its focus on humanitarian aid; and the children may possibly find that they can recycle some of the facts and figures that they used in that exercise. More importantly, I find it a more challenging subject than the frequently-set theme of the dangers of smoking. It seems to me that the latter subject does not require a great deal of creative thought – there is really only one direction in which the essay can go; very few people these days would argue that smoking is a good and perfectly safe thing to do.

Overseas Aid, on the other hand, can be a contentious issue. In my experience of teaching this workshop, I have found that children can be quite divided on the subject: while many believe strongly in providing help to people in the developing world, others are of the opinion that charity should begin at home. This can lead to quite animated debate during class discussions prior to writing the essays – and heated emotions can often spark creativity.

And there is another benefit: one of the persuasive techniques the children will be learning about is stating the opposing point of view to the one that you are making, and then refuting it. If both sides of the argument are being voiced in the classroom, pupils will have the opposing viewpoint presented to them on a plate, so to speak. All they will then need to do is work out how to demolish the opposition's argument effectively!

The pupils will need to do some preparation for this workshop: researching the subject – for example via government and charity websites – to find the information and statistics they may need in order to make their case: How much do we spend on Overseas Aid? What is it spent on? Who receives it? What are the benefits? What are the arguments for and against? etc. No doubt they would be grateful for some advice from the teacher or workshop leader on which websites or publications might be a good source of information!

Beginning and ending

Start the lesson by reminding the pupils of the two ways to begin and five ways to end – hopefully, by this stage they shouldn't need much reminding. Ask them what their Key Point is; it will almost certainly be the main thrust of their argument, something like:

■ we have a duty to help people in poorer parts of the world by providing Overseas Aid; or

- there are lots of poor people in this country; we should help them before we help people overseas.

Should they use this Key Point to begin their essay? Or should they lead up to it by using a Tease Opening along the lines of:

> In this country, some people consider themselves poor if they can't afford designer trainers or the latest video game. But in parts of the developing world, poverty means something quite different. It means not having enough food, no clean water, no health care. For many people in poorer countries, Overseas Aid from wealthier nations like ours can mean the difference between life and death – and I think it is our duty to help them.

An opening like that draws the reader in before hitting them with the Key Point; Tease Openings can be very persuasive.

An alternative way of teasing the reader at the start would be to *use a brief story which illustrates your Key Point* – for example, a couple of lines about a little boy or girl who is dying for lack of medicine and whose best chance of survival is Overseas Aid. That would be the written equivalent of what we did in the poster, when we used a photograph and a child's story to personalise our message and stir the readers' imagination.

Whatever type of opening the pupils choose to employ, it should be something that grabs the readers' attention and makes them want to read on. And the ending should bring the essay to a satisfying conclusion and reinforce the message we want to put across. Any one of the five endings that the pupils have learned can be effective in achieving this – but it is worth pointing out to them that if they choose to begin their essay with a brief story, then they might well find that a Circular Ending would be appropriate and highly effective. An essay that began with the story of a child whose life depended on Overseas Aid – as in the example above – could be brought to a very powerful conclusion by referring to the child again and saying that Overseas Aid gives him a chance of life; without it, he will probably not live to see his next birthday.

Having thought about how they will begin and end, the children need to consider the middle part of their essay. They should have all the information they need in order to back up their argument, but how do they make that argument effective? How do they convince the reader that their opinion is the correct one? They need to learn a few …

Persuasive writing techniques

Writers can't *force* people to agree with them, but by phrasing things in certain ways and employing a few psychological tricks, they can hopefully *persuade* them. Three effective ways of getting people to agree with you are:

- Make statements that no one could disagree with.
- Mention opposing arguments and counter them.
- Save your best argument till last.
- Pose questions and then answer them.

Here are some examples of how those might work:

Make statements that no one could disagree with

'Nobody wants to see a child die.' Who could deny that? Your reader is forced to agree with you, so then you link that statement to a point in favour of your argument, continuing along the lines of: 'Yet each year thousands/hundreds of thousands/millions of them do, because they don't have enough food/medicines/clean water. Overseas Aid can stop them dying – and that's something we all want.' Your argument is made!

Mention opposing arguments and counter them

If you were arguing the case *for* Overseas Aid, it would be a good tactic to make a statement giving the opposite point of view – 'There are plenty of poor people in this country – perhaps *they* should be our priority' – and then go on to shoot that argument down by continuing ... 'But they're not starving; they're not dying for lack of basic medicines; their homes haven't been destroyed by civil war.' By using this technique, you give the impression that you have given the matter a great deal of thought and weighed up all the pros and cons. You are not trying to hide the fact that there are arguments against – far from it; you are openly acknowledging them. You are aware of these arguments, you have considered them carefully – but you have rejected them. Using this technique makes you sound confident; it gives the impression that you are right and the other side is wrong.

Save your best argument till last

When young people go to a gig, they wouldn't expect the headline act to appear first. There are usually supporting acts which set the mood and get the audience warmed up before the big star appears. The gig builds towards a climax – and that's what a piece of writing should do. The final argument should have a real impact – that's the one that will be freshest in the readers' minds when they come to the end of the piece, so it needs to be a really effective one that will clinch the case you are making.

Pose questions and then answer them

This technique can be used for putting a point across – 'And what was the result? Nearly half a million people left homeless!' – or for countering an opposing argument: 'Why don't the governments in those countries help their own people? They *do* – but they just don't have enough money to do everything that's needed.' It's an effective way of engaging with your readers; it's like being there in the room with them asking them a question. It makes them feel as if you're appealing to them personally – and that makes it more likely that they will agree with you.

Style

Before they begin writing their essays, give the children a couple of pointers on style. The first one has been said before – it first reared its head in Chapter 7, but it's worth repeating:

Short, clear sentences are far better than long, rambling ones.

The second one, though, will be new to them, and may come as a surprise:

Don't overload your essay with statistics.

Statistics add weight to your argument, but if you use too many of them, they can become rather boring and make your readers switch off. The answer is to use them sparingly, so that the essay is not a jumble of numbers, but rather a flowing, engaging, highly readable, incredibly *persuasive* piece of work.
Hopefully.

Fiction – advanced

11

Advanced character creation

In Chapter 4, we got the class to create interesting and believable Main Characters by thinking in great detail about their daily lives, their likes and dislikes, character traits, family, background and so on. But it is not enough just to make the main protagonist believable – *all the characters in a story must be well-rounded*, and in this chapter we will be looking at how to get that message across.

We will also be revisiting and expanding on Back Story, set-up and motivation, which were first introduced in Chapter 2; discussing the roles of *protagonists and antagonists*; and showing how putting characters under pressure by presenting them with *dilemmas* can not only produce moments of high drama, but also provide insights into the true nature of our characters.

All characters must be well-rounded

Our Main Character, or protagonist, is the person who will carry the story along, and so we must identify with them and find them interesting and believable. But other characters will have a significant part to play, too; if they *aren't* important to the story, why bother including them? Some of the action will revolve around them, they may provide obstacles to the protagonist or be the means of him or her overcoming obstacles, and if they are merely cardboard cut-outs, the story will lose a lot of its effectiveness.

A good way of getting young people to appreciate the importance of making all characters well-rounded is to get the class talking about a TV show which all of them will surely know – *The Simpsons*. Start by asking them: 'Who is your favourite character from *The Simpsons*?' You will probably get virtually the entire cast-list – children love showing off how well they know a TV series – and the fact that every one is *someone's* favourite shows how each and every one of the characters has been given qualities that make them interesting and appealing to viewers. They all have distinctive personalities – and to illustrate how well the children know them, try putting this scenario to them and asking them how the characters will react:

A beer wagon (the class will usually supply the extra information that it would be a Duff beer wagon!) is driving through the streets of Springfield. It hits a bump and a barrel of beer falls off. Homer finds it – so what does he do?:

1. Report it to the police?
2. Phone the Duff brewery to tell them about it?
3. Keep it?

Every child who has seen *The Simpsons* would know that Homer would keep it – so now ask them how other characters would react to this fact.

■ *Would Barney think Homer had done the right thing?* (Yes, he would. In fact, he'd be hoping that Homer would share it with him!)

■ *Would Ned Flanders?* (No, certainly not! He'd give Homer a lecture – though a very diplomatic one – on the virtues of honesty.)

■ *If Marge found out, would she think Homer ought to give the beer back?* (Yes, she would.)

■ *Would Bart?* (No, he'd think Homer did the right thing.)

■ *So what sort of thing would Bart say? Something like 'Nice one, Dad'?* (The class will probably correct you here – Bart doesn't call him 'Dad', he usually calls him 'Homer'.)

■ *Would Lisa approve of Homer's behaviour?* (No, she'd disapprove forcefully.)

■ *So would Lisa say 'You should give it back, Homer'?* (No doubt the class will tell you that she wouldn't call him 'Homer', she'd say 'Dad'.)

This exercise should prove to the class that they know *The Simpsons* characters really well – they know how they would react to a given situation, and even the sort of language they would use. This is because *all the characters are very well-rounded.* The writers of the programme have taken care to create a whole army of believable and consistent characters. It's not just the main characters who are well-written, it's *every* character. And this is crucial to the success of the show, because at some stage in some episode, each of the characters is likely to be the focus of a storyline and have an important role to play – and they need to be well-rounded in order to carry it off.

And this is not just true of *The Simpsons*: think of all the characters in *The Lord of the Rings* and the Harry Potter books; think of TV soap operas. Characters who play a minor role in a story – in film and TV parlance, those with 'walk-on' parts – don't need a vast amount of attention; they can usually be painted in fairly broad brush-strokes. But every character who plays a significant part needs to be given a believable, well-thought-out and interesting personality.

Back Story revisited (with exercise)

Back Story has an important part to play when we are creating characters because, as we have seen, someone's personality – the way they think and act, the way they *are* – has been shaped by things that have happened to them in the past.

Each of our characters should have a Back Story – but how do we set about giving them one? Well, when we are creating a character, we will usually know the role we want them to play – the so-called friend who betrays our heroine; the property developer who wants to close down the cottage hospital; the inspirational sports coach who helps our hero qualify for the Olympics; etc. They will have certain personality traits, either attractive or repellent, and we need to ask ourselves: 'How did he or she get to *be* like that?' In other words, what happened to them in the past that has made them the way they are? What is their Back Story?

Here's an exercise to help the class get the hang of creating a Back Story: in Chapter 2 we looked at Cinderella's life in the years leading up to the start of the story – and now our focus switches to the Wicked Stepmother. She is clearly a nasty character, and the example she sets to the Ugly Sisters has made them pretty unpleasant, too. Yet, presumably, she wasn't *born* wicked – it's hard to imagine a thoroughly wicked baby! So something about her upbringing, or something that happened to her, must have *made* her wicked. What was it?

The children's task is to create a Back Story for the Wicked Stepmother, which explains why she turned out the way she did. Allow them about 15–20 minutes, preferably working in groups, to write a brief outline of her life, including one particular incident which had a profound effect on her and was instrumental in setting her on the path of wickedness. When they have finished, get the groups to read their outlines to the rest of the class for comment and constructive criticism.

This exercise should help reinforce an important point to the class: as a general rule, *people don't behave the way they do for no reason.* There is nearly always an explanation for their behaviour, and it is usually to be found somewhere in their Back Story, which is why creating one for every significant character is so useful. We may refer to it at some point during the story or we may not, but a logical Back Story makes a character more consistent, more believable, more real – not just to the reader, but to the writer, too.

Just before we leave the subject of Back Story, it might be relevant to mention the 2010 film *Robin Hood*, starring Russell Crowe. It's an interesting take on the Robin Hood legend, in that it doesn't deal with Robin's adventures with his Merry Men in Sherwood Forest; instead it sets out to create a Back Story for the legend. The writers have clearly asked themselves how Robin came to be an outlaw, living in the forest with Maid Marion, Little John, Friar Tuck and the rest, fighting for justice on behalf of the downtrodden peasants – and in answering those questions they have come up with the entire plot of a film, which ends with the caption: 'And so the legend begins.' This version of Robin Hood is Back Story writ large – and it might be instructive for the pupils to watch it, if they have the chance.

More about set-up

Again, this is something which was touched upon in Chapter 2 – but now let's look at set-up in a little more depth.

If a character suddenly does something that we had no idea he was able to do, we find it confusing: we didn't know about this remarkable ability. It appears to us that the writer has made this up on the spur of the moment in order to help the character deal with a tricky situation – and in the case of young authors, that's often the case. In order to make it believable, the fact that the character *has* this ability must be flagged up in advance; there needs to be a set-up.

To demonstrate to the children how this can be achieved, try engaging them in a class discussion about the film *Mrs Doubtfire*. It's a reasonable assumption that more of them will have seen the film than will have read Anne Fine's novel *Madame Doubtfire* on which it was based – so we're going to focus on the movie version.

In order to reinforce what the class have learned about the Obstacles Structure, begin by asking them a few questions about the structure of the film, focusing on the Main Character Daniel, played by Robin Williams:

- *What is Daniel's objective in the story – what is his journey?* The type of answer we are looking for is that he wants to spend more time with his children. At present his access to them is very limited, due to divorce proceedings.

- *What is the Inciting Incident that enables him to begin his journey?* His wife advertises for a housekeeper.

- *What are the obstacles that prevent Daniel from applying for the job?* Obviously his wife will not contemplate making him her housekeeper – she thinks he's a bad influence on the children. And for another thing, she wants a female housekeeper.

Daniel could overcome those obstacles if he could disguise himself as a woman – but he would need to be totally convincing. He would have to fool his wife and his children, and that would be virtually impossible for most ordinary men. *But* – we know that Daniel is no ordinary man.

At the beginning of the film we saw him at work, providing the voices for characters in a cartoon. It seemed that the purpose of this scene was to establish him as a funny, quirky, likeable sort of person – making him a sympathetic character that the audience would identify with. But it had another purpose, too: it showed us that he was good at putting on accents and that he had lots of acting ability.

A little later in the film we see him with his brother, who works in the film industry, specialising in make-up and prosthetics that are incredibly realistic. Knowing about his brother's skill and Daniel's own talent for acting, we are not surprised when he is able to dress up as Mrs Doubtfire and get the housekeeper's job. We are totally convinced – as are Daniel's wife and children – because his ability to carry it off has been set up in advance.

The occasional need for a set-up is a strong argument in favour of writing an outline before going on to tackle the full story. Looking through the outline with a critical eye, the writer should be able to identify things which need to be set up in advance, and amend the outline accordingly. Discovering the need for a set-up part-way through writing the story, and then having to go back and shoe-horn in additional scenes or incidents, is far less satisfactory.

Creating motivation (with exercise)

As we have seen, characters should have a motive for doing what they do – otherwise, why would they do it? Daniel disguising himself as Mrs Doubtfire is great fun and leads to lots of funny and dramatic situations – but why would he go to all that trouble if he didn't hope to gain something by it? In *The Lord of the Rings*, why would Frodo undertake such a perilous journey, unless there were very good reasons for doing so? If he *doesn't* take the ring to Mount Doom, the whole of Middle Earth will be enslaved by Sauron; the consequences of not doing it are too awful to contemplate – so he has an excellent motive.

Characters can have all sorts of reasons for behaving in certain ways and doing certain things, including:

- fear (physical fear, fear of detection, fear of failure, fear of consequences);
- love;
- hatred;

- jealousy;
- revenge;
- desperation;
- ambition;
- to escape something.

We can give the class some practice in creating motivation by setting them this exercise:

Get them to imagine that they are writing a movie based on the story of Cinderella. The film's producer – a very kind-hearted woman – decides that she wants a happy ending, not just for Cinderella and the Prince, but also for the Ugly Sisters. So when the Prince arrives at the house to try the slipper on the sisters, she wants them to say: 'We're sure it won't fit us, but it will probably fit our beautiful sister.' And Cinderella tries the slipper on, and the Sisters congratulate her, and she's thrilled that they are being nice to her, and asks them to come and live with her and the Prince at the palace.

Now, that gives our young writers a bit of a problem. They have written lots of scenes showing the Ugly Sisters to be vain, selfish and spiteful, so being kind to Cinderella and encouraging the Prince to marry her is totally out of character for them. How do they make this believable?

The class's task is to write an extra scene, to be inserted earlier in the story, which provides the Ugly Sisters with a motive for giving up their own ambitions to marry the Prince. They can include additional characters, if necessary.

Allow them about 15 minutes to sketch out the scene, and then have a class discussion about the ideas they have come up with. You may wish to create a scene outline of your own – or you may prefer to offer them this solution:

> It is the evening of the Ball, and the Ugly Sisters corner the Prince during a break between dances, and try to chat him up. They say that it must be wonderful being a Prince or Princess, but the Prince replies that it isn't easy being the heir to the throne: it involves a lot of hard work and devotion to duty, and he rarely has any time to himself. His younger brother has lots more fun – all the luxury and none of the work; it's much better to be a relative of the heir to the throne rather than actually being the heir. This leads the Ugly Sisters to think that if Cinderella marries the Prince and they're friendly with her, they can live a life of luxury at the Palace and never do a stroke of work. One of them may even get to marry the Prince's younger brother and become a Princess after all.

Adding this scene to the story would give the Ugly Sisters an excellent motive for encouraging Cinderella to marry the Prince, and the kind-hearted producer would be satisfied.

Protagonist versus antagonist

In looking at the plot of Cinderella in such detail, we have had a great deal to say about the Wicked Stepmother and the Ugly Sisters, because they are such an important part of the story. Cinderella is the heroine; the 'goodie'; the protagonist – and they are the villains; the 'baddies'; the antagonists, with the Wicked Stepmother being the main one.

When writing stories, the children will find it extremely useful to include one or more antagonists: they can be a major source of obstacles, and the fact that they are working in opposition to the protagonist gives plenty of scope for conflict, which is a key ingredient of drama. And if they are a bit quirky and seem to really *enjoy* being wicked – like Cruella De Vil in *101 Dalmatians* or the various 'baddies' in the Batman films – villains can be quite attractive characters and are often great fun to write.

A question I am often asked in workshops is: 'Can the antagonist be the Main Character?' And it's a difficult one to answer. Without wishing to delve too deeply into the origins of words, 'antagonist' has its roots in 'anti' – against. The antagonist ought to be *opposing* someone or something – that's the nature of the beast. Their role is to work against the protagonist.

And yet that can be switched around to a certain extent if the villain's evil schemes are so awful and ambitious that they dominate the story, and the hero's journey is all about thwarting them – so he or she is the one finding ways to place obstacles that will prevent the villain from succeeding. An example of this can be found in *The Lord of the Rings*, where the overarching aim of all the 'goodies' is to prevent Sauron from enslaving the whole of Middle Earth. Sauron may be an extremely significant character, but he's still not the protagonist of the story.

So perhaps the best answer to young writers asking the above question is: 'Stick to having a sympathetic Main Character as your protagonist – you'll find it easier – but put plenty of effort into creating a truly memorable villain.' Hopefully, that should satisfy them!

If it doesn't, you could perhaps suggest that they make their protagonist *flawed* rather than outright wicked – an *anti-hero*: someone who is not exactly a 'goodie', but who is fascinating and has redeeming features that make them attractive to the reader. Older pupils will probably be familiar with 'The Man With No Name', the character played by Clint Eastwood in spaghetti westerns – an anti-hero, if ever there was one.

Dilemmas (with exercise)

When characters have difficult decisions to make, we learn a lot about them. When faced with an agonising dilemma they are under pressure, often out of their comfort zone, and the choices they make reveal a great deal about their true personality. Are they brave or cowardly? Selfless or selfish? Clever or stupid?

An excellent example of this emerged during one of my workshops, when the class were discussing possible storylines for Cinderella II, and you should find it useful as the basis for a class discussion. Here's the situation:

> The King and Queen – Prince Charming's parents – are kidnapped during an attack on the palace. The kidnappers send a note to the Prince, saying that his parents will be killed unless a ransom is paid. And the sum is enormous – the entire wealth of the kingdom. What should Prince Charming do? If he pays up, he will probably get his parents back safely, but the kingdom will be bankrupted, the people might starve and he will have lost his inheritance. If he *doesn't* pay, it's likely that his parents will be killed – but that would mean he would become king himself and inherit all the wealth of the kingdom.

It's a terrible dilemma – and the way he reacts to it will be very revealing. What is more important to him – his parents, his lifestyle, his ambitions, his people? What does Cinderella think he should do? The advice she gives to the Prince will say a great deal about her, as well.

When the class have discussed this – and if my experiences are anything to go by, it's likely to be a very animated debate! – then get them to think about another, more modern dilemma:

> A boy's parents split up when he was two years old. The father walked out and set up home with someone else, and disappeared from the boy's life completely – he never even sent a birthday card. The boy's mother struggled to bring up her son on her own; there was never much money, but there was a lot of love in the household. Ten years later, the boy's father got back in touch. He'd built up a successful business and made lots of money; he wanted his son to come and live with him in his big house, and said that he would give him everything money could buy. The boy's mother was appalled, but said that the decision was up to the boy; she didn't want to stand in his way. The boy was very tempted by everything his father had to offer, but he loved his

mother very much and was truly grateful for everything she had done for him.

What should the boy do? And what would the children's decision be if this happened to them?

Hopefully those two examples will have demonstrated to the class how much drama can be achieved by putting characters under pressure and presenting them with a dilemma. So now, get them to try it out for themselves with the following writing exercise:

1. Create a character.
2. Write the outline of a scene in which that character is faced with a dilemma.
3. Consider the pros and cons of the various decisions that the character might make.
4. Say what the character eventually decides to do – and what that reveals about him or her.

As ever, a class discussion of their efforts would be extremely useful.

A common fault in children's writing is that they channel most of their efforts into creating an exciting plot, and then populate it with characters who are little more than cardboard cut-outs. Hopefully, the things that have been discussed and practised in this chapter will show them that interesting, engaging and realistic characters are an essential ingredient of any story. If they learn to think of them as real people with real backgrounds and real emotions, their writing will be all the better for it.

12

Advanced structure

In the previous chapter, we talked about the importance of giving all our significant characters well-rounded personalities, and now we'll be showing the children why this is necessary as we deal with *multiple Character Journeys*. We will also learn more about how to structure writing. The Obstacles Structure was introduced right at the beginning as a way of getting children to think about how stories are put together, and now we're going to build on that by introducing them to the classic *3-act structure*, and also show pupils a way of giving a natural dramatic flow to their writing by following a template that I call *the Seasons Structure*.

Multiple Character Journeys

When we first dealt with Character Journeys back in Chapter 1, referring to the story of Cinderella, we focused on just one journey: our main protagonist's. Yet most stories will feature a number of significant characters, as we have seen – and *each one will have their own journey*. It may well not be as long or as detailed as the Main Character's, but it will be a journey nonetheless.

A good way to illustrate this is to initiate a class discussion about the 1993 film *Cool Runnings*. Very popular with young people, it's a film that the children may well know – but if they don't, it doesn't really matter; you can always describe it to them.

It's the story of four young men who get together to form Jamaica's first-ever bobsled team, under the guidance of an American coach, played by John Candy. In this film, although the coach is the person driving the plot along, it is arguably the *group as a whole* who acts as the protagonist, rather than an individual, and the group who has the journey – which is to represent their country in the Winter Olympics. But each member of the group has a different motivation for taking part:

- One of them is seeking to emulate his father, who competed in the Olympics.

- Another wants to broaden his horizons, get away from Jamaica and see the world.

- The third team member feels the need to assert his independence and stop being dominated by his overbearing father.

- The fourth one is out to have fun and show the world that Jamaicans are cool.

- The team's coach needs to redeem himself after being disqualified for cheating in a previous Olympics.

With these five different motivations, there are five individual Character Journeys taking place within the overall group journey – and the obstacles that hamper those individual journeys affect the overall journey, too.

In the film, the team achieve their aim of qualifying for the Olympics, and surprise everyone by doing well in the competition. They don't win a medal – a crash due to mechanical failure puts paid to that – but they impress a lot of people. And as the film draws to a close, it is clear that they have gained acceptance when a member of one of the top teams tells them: 'We'll see you in four years' time' – a good example of an ending that hints of further developments. We know now that this was not a one-off for the Jamaican bobsled team; they will keep on practising and improving, and they will be ready to give everyone a run for their money at the next Olympics.

The group's journey has been a successful one – and so have the individual journeys of the team members:

- The first one *has* followed in his father's footsteps.

- The second one has seen the world, though he no longer feels the need to escape from Jamaica.

- The third has faced up to his domineering father and earned his respect.

- The fourth has given the team a cool, laid-back style that is typically Jamaican.

- The coach has won back the respect of Olympic officials.

And all the different threads have been woven together into one absorbing, entertaining and very satisfying story. It would be a good idea to encourage the class to watch the film while all this talk of Character Journeys is still fresh in their minds; I doubt if they would find it an objectionable task!

Multiple journeys like the ones in *Cool Runnings* are fairly common. You will find them in just about every story that features two or more people who have a common aim but a variety of different agendas – groups, gangs, teams, *Three Men in a Boat*, *The Magnificent Seven*, *Ocean's Eleven* and so on.

The Lord of the Rings is another good example to talk through with the class. How many different Character Journeys does that contain? Ask the pupils to name some of the characters and think about what their journeys are. In particular, get them to focus on:

■ Frodo and Sam;

■ Aragorn;

■ Gandalf;

■ Boromir.

All of these Character Journeys interconnect frequently during the story – and at one stage all five characters start out together on a joint journey as members of the Fellowship of the Ring. But they all have individual objectives and – in the case of Boromir – they are not all pulling in the same direction.

And then get the class to think about the journeys of two characters working in opposition to the protagonists – the antagonists Sauron and Saruman. The fact that their journeys are running counter to those of the protagonists provides most of the conflict, jeopardy and drama of the story.

They are clearly the 'baddies', while Frodo, Sam, Aragorn and Gandalf are 'goodies'. But how would we describe Gollum (or Sméagol)? He is an obstacle some of the time, but helpful on other occasions – and he is the final means of destroying the ring when Frodo has decided to hold on to it. He is something of a split personality: baddie *and* goodie, Gollum *and* Sméagol – with a journey that sometimes runs alongside Frodo's and sometimes runs counter to it, creating obstacles.

Multiple journeys are one of the main reasons why writers need to put a great deal of thought into *all* their characters, not just the main protagonist. Each one of them is likely to have a journey that will impact on the story, so each one of them must be well-rounded, believable and interesting.

But, of course, juggling a large number of Character Journeys which all interconnect takes a great deal of writing skill, and it is not something that the novice writer is likely to be capable of. So let's set the class a somewhat easier task – *writing two Character Journeys* that run in opposition to each other, in other words the journeys of a *protagonist* and an *antagonist*.

Two journeys – protagonist and antagonist exercise

As discussed in the previous chapter, the main antagonist in the Cinderella story is the Wicked Stepmother – but what would the class say is her journey? It could probably be summed up in this way: *to marry one of her daughters off to the Prince*. This is a journey that we hope will fail, because if it is successful, then Cinderella's dreams of finding true love and escaping from drudgery will come to nothing. The two journeys are interlinked.

The Wicked Stepmother's journey has the same Inciting Incident as Cinderella's – the invitation to the ball – but there are different obstacles in her path: the fact that her daughters are ugly, unpleasant and vain is something that threatens the success of her scheme, but the main obstacle is Cinderella herself. If she wins the Prince's heart, then the stepmother's journey will end in failure, which is why she does everything she can to keep the Prince and Cinderella apart.

So we have two main Character Journeys – protagonist v. antagonist; heroine v. villain; goodie v. baddie – and the way in which they oppose each other is central to the plot. The class's task is now to come up with the outline of a story which incorporates these elements:

- Two journeys – one for the protagonist and one for the antagonist.
- The journeys should interconnect and may even share the same Inciting Incident, as was the case with Cinderella and the Wicked Stepmother.
- The reader would want one journey to succeed and the other one to fail.
- Each of the characters should have a motive for achieving their goal.

The class may want a few ideas to get them started, so how about these?:

The characters may have the same goal – they may want the same thing for different reasons: one may want it for a good purpose, the other for a bad purpose. Their goal might be an object; money; to win someone's affections; to save something that is threatened; to be the first to make a significant discovery. They may be competing against each other in some way. The antagonist may be placing obstacles in the way of the protagonist for whatever reason; or it may be that the protagonist's journey is to thwart the evil designs of the antagonist by putting obstacles in his or her way.

Once the outlines are written, get the class to discuss them and offer constructive criticism, as before. Perhaps you would like them to go on and write these stories, or you may consider that writing an outline is sufficient. If you wanted to give them further practice, you might suggest that they *add a third Character Journey*, which is connected to the others – perhaps an ally of the protagonist or a sidekick of the antagonist. If you *do* want them to write the story in full, then it might be worth pointing out to them that they don't necessarily need to devote equal time to the two separate journeys in their story. They will probably want to focus on their protagonist, while the antagonist's journey is progressing in the background and only coming to the forefront when it directly affects the hero or heroine. Cinderella and the Wicked Stepmother don't get equal billing!

Writing stories that require multiple Character Journeys is not easy, especially for the novice writer. But once they have mastered the basics, children can gradually build up the number of Character Journeys in their stories, as their writing skills grow. In time – who knows? – they might find that they could confidently tackle *Five Children and It ... The Magnificent Seven ... The Dirty Dozen ...* even *Ocean's Thirteen*. Or, at least they could if those hadn't already been written!

The 3-act structure

The 3-act structure has certainly stood the test of time: Aristotle propounded the view of a story being played out in three stages back in the fourth century BC, and it has been a staple of dramatic structure ever since. The three stages are basically 'beginning', 'middle' and 'end', and the acts can be broken down like this:

Act 1 sets the scene, introduces the characters – notably the protagonist – and includes an event that gets the plot under way.

Act 2 develops the plot through various complications and setbacks, building the drama and tension until the story reaches

Act 3, in which the plot reaches its climax, followed by a brief denouement.

Let's look at how that fits in with what the children have come to know as the Obstacles Structure. We have talked about the need to set up the characters and situation early on, and have shown how the Inciting Incident triggers the character's journey, so Act 1 is covered. Placing obstacles for the protagonist to overcome provides the complications as the plot develops in Act 2, with False Horizon moments adding to the tension before the journey is completed in Act 3. As for the denouement, that was covered in Chapter 5, when we suggested that the children end their stories with a brief paragraph or scene showing the effects of the journey. But we didn't linger on it, and we didn't give it its proper name – so perhaps it's time to talk about the *denouement* in a little more detail.

If they watch films – and which child doesn't? – they will very likely know what a denouement is already, without being aware that it has a special name. It's that scene which takes place after the story has reached its climax, which hints at some of the consequences of what has happened and ties up any loose ends. All the drama and conflict is over; it's like the lull *after* the storm.

In *Cool Runnings*, back in Jamaica after the Games, we see the man whose father was an Olympic champion putting a photo of the bobsled team next to a picture of his father's triumph; at the end of *Mrs Doubtfire*, we see Daniel picking his children up from school, after his wife has relented over the custody issues; if we were writing a story about the fight to save a cottage hospital, as touched upon in the previous chapter, we might end with a celebration party at the hospital.

The denouement needn't be too long – after all, the story is effectively over – and the one in Cinderella is very brief indeed: it's really just the words 'And they lived happily ever after.' One that *is* very long is to be found at the end of 'The Return of the King', the final part of *The Lord of the Rings* trilogy, and it might be instructive to ask the class what they think of it. After the destruction of the ring, the quest is fulfilled and the main part of the story is over. But because there have been so many Character Journeys, there are an awful lot of loose ends to be tied up, so we have:

- The crowning of Aragorn as King.
- Frodo and the other hobbits returning to the Shire and having to deal with lots of problems there.
- Many of the major characters leaving for the Grey Havens.

The denouement of *The Lord of the Rings* has been criticised in some quarters for going on too long – what is the class's view? Is it really necessary to have all that action after the main journey is over? Could they come up with any alternatives?

The 3-act structure may be the classic guide to putting a story together, but it's not the only one: there's the 4-act structure, the 5-act structure, and some people swear by the 7-act structure. I don't propose to go into any of those here – it would over-complicate things, and the class can explore those structures if they wish once they are established and successful writers. Instead, let's introduce them to a concept that they should, hopefully, find useful in giving a strong dramatic flow to their stories – a concept that I call the Seasons Structure.

The Seasons Structure

As the name suggests, it's based on the natural cycle of the seasons as one leads into another – and that flow is echoed in lots of stories:

Spring – a time of new beginnings and the promise of good things to come.
Summer – a time of fulfilment; everything is wonderful.
Autumn – the first chill winds start to blow, indicating that the good times may not continue.
Winter – a bleak time; the optimism of Spring and the fulfilment of Summer seem long gone.

And that's where the story might end, in the case of a tragedy. But in a more optimistic, happy-ending type of story, the cycle is continued so that Winter is followed once again by ...

Spring – the dawning of fresh hope; the bad times may be over; there is a brighter future ahead.

Let's look at how that might apply if we were wanting to write a story about a young man with dreams of becoming a rock star. He forms a band and starts to climb the ladder of success, with the flow of the plot mirroring the seasons:

■ Spring – people start to recognise his and the band's talent, they build up a fan base and are offered a recording contract.
■ Summer – the band really takes off and they become major stars who can fill stadiums.
■ Autumn – spoiled by success, he develops a drink or drugs habit, his behaviour becomes erratic.
■ Winter – gigs get cancelled because he fails to show up, the record company drops the band, they split up; he ends up being given a prison sentence.

But we wouldn't want the story to end there, so we continue the cycle by moving on to ...

■ Spring – shocked at how things have turned out, he kicks his drink/drugs habit, sorts out his life and starts to make a comeback.

In the case of a love story, using the Seasons Structure might result in this:

- Spring – the couple meet and fall in love.
- Summer – they are blissfully happy.
- Autumn – they start to argue and problems escalate.
- Winter – they decide they are incompatible and separate.
- Spring – they can't live without each other and rebuild their relationship, and this time it is stronger.

To make sure the class have grasped the concept, see if they can spot *how the Seasons Structure relates to Cinderella*. Mention in advance that the seasons don't need to be too long – in fact, one phase of the story moves through three seasons in just a few hours. We start by asking:

> In which season does the story start?

It begins in Winter. It's true that in the Disney version, Cinderella is shown singing happily and interacting with her friends the animals – but that is just a device to portray her as a sunny, optimistic character and make us empathise with her. Underneath the cheerful façade, Cinderella's life is bleak: she is an orphan who is being bullied and forced to act as an unpaid servant to her stepmother and stepsisters, and there seems to be no prospect of her life changing for the better.

> When does Spring begin?

The invitation to the ball brings the dawning of hope, the prospect of escaping drudgery for one night at least ... and possibly more. Winter is not entirely behind her – there are still some setbacks ahead, in the form of the early obstacles which are placed in her way – but the overall mood is upbeat and optimistic.

> What about Summer and Autumn?

When she arrives at the ball and the Prince is smitten by her, it feels like Summer. As the couple dance and fall in love, it is as if the sun is shining on them both. But then Autumn arrives with the chiming of the clock at midnight. The chill winds of reality change the mood completely. It appears that the golden times cannot last forever.

How does the cycle continue?

As she weeps in the kitchen afterwards, with all her hopes and dreams shattered, it is Winter again for Cinderella. But, of course, the Spring will always return – and sure enough, it does as the Prince finally tracks her down and asks her to marry him. And the story ends at the beginning of Summer, with the prospect of many wonderful days ahead as Cinderella and the Prince live happily ever after.

Did the class spot where the short seasons came? On the night of the ball, she went from Summer to Autumn to Winter in just a couple of hours. It's not the length of the seasons that's important, but the *flow*; the sequence of ...

- optimism;
- fulfilment;
- disappointment/disillusion;
- despair;
- renewed hope.

... is a very effective dramatic structure.

The Seasons Structure can be used for the whole story, or for segments within it. There are no rules about which season to start in, but probably the best two are the seasons we used for the examples given above: Spring and Winter. It doesn't suit *all* stories, but young writers often find it extremely useful when they are thinking about how to construct their plots.

And after telling them all this, get the class to try it out for themselves by setting them an *exercise* – writing the outline of a story which follows the Seasons Structure.

Different types of structure – ones not covered in this book – are things that young people can experiment with as their writing skills develop, if they so choose; for those with literary ambitions there is plenty of information out there. But perhaps the best way they can improve their mastery of story structure is to read books, watch plays, films and television programmes, try to analyse how the story is put together and see if there is a structure or a technique there that they can use in their own writing. Writers can always learn something from the work of others.

13

Scriptwriting

I wouldn't recommend that children try their hand at writing scripts until they are reasonably adept at prose stories and have a fair command of character and story structure. They will need to have mastered the basics, because when they tackle scriptwriting they will have to take the skills they have already acquired and start using them in a rather different way. They will need to start thinking about stories in more visual terms than they have previously – *showing* rather than *telling*.

This is well illustrated by the extract from Alan Bennett's book *Untold Stories* which was quoted in Chapter 9 as part of a non-fiction lesson. It was the author's idea for the opening scene of a film – and it is extremely visual. If the class have not tackled that particular lesson, then I would suggest that you read that scene to them before teaching them about scriptwriting, to show them how a master of the craft plans a script; the way in which he *visualises*.

Scriptwriting will present the children with a new set of challenges, and in this chapter we'll be showing them how to handle two of the most basic ones. First and foremost, instead of writing prose, they will be *writing dialogue* – and of course the spoken word is different from the written word. So we will be giving them some tips on how to make their dialogue sound realistic. They will also have to start thinking about *telling a story through scenes* that move the plot along and keep the audience involved and entertained – and we will be showing them how to set about that.

Once they have acquired those two skills, they should be able to write a fairly basic script. They are unlikely to be good enough to worry Alan Bennett, but they will be off and running. And if they show an aptitude for scriptwriting, or if they are an older or particularly gifted class, then you can introduce them to some of the more advanced scriptwriting skills described in the next chapter. But for most children, the mysteries of subtext and exposition can be put to one side for the time being, while they focus on the basics.

Writing dialogue

Books and stories often contain dialogue, but because it's meant to be read rather than listened to, it doesn't matter too much if it's a bit clunky (which it often is). In a script, it matters a lot. So how do we make sure our dialogue is realistic and sounds right? Easy!:

Speak dialogue out loud as you're writing it.

As I write those words, I can visualise teachers throughout the land howling in anguish at the prospect of large numbers of pupils all gabbling away in the classroom as they write their scripts – but honestly, it's the one fool-proof way of ensuring authentic dialogue. When I was a young television staff writer, I was part of a team writing scripts for the TV station announcers, and we always spoke our scripts out loud as we were writing them. The constant hubbub in the office never affected our concentration, and the scripts were well-nigh perfect replications of natural speech. I rest my case.

Perhaps children writing in a classroom could be encouraged to *mutter* their dialogue or whisper it to themselves, but only if they speak it in some way will they know if it sounds convincing. And having let that particular genie out of the bottle, I'm prepared to go further:

If the character you're writing for has an accent of some kind, then use that accent to speak the dialogue.

For example, take this line of dialogue: 'I wouldn't *dream* of doing that! It's wrong!'

It sounds fine – but if the character it was written for happened to come from another country and had a foreign accent, they might well speak more formally and say: 'I would not *dream* of doing that! It is wrong!'

Try it in various accents and you'll see what I mean. Issues like that are not apparent when you look at dialogue written down on the page – you only become aware of them when the words are spoken.

Dialogue should sound natural, and it should also fit the character it is written for. Try reading these lines to the class; they both say the same thing, but in different ways:

> 'She'd been spreading these awful rumours about me, and then she had the nerve to ask me if I'd lend her some money. I just said no, straight to her face.'

'She'd been bad-mouthing me all over the place, and then she goes and asks me to lend her some money. I was like, no way!'

Which of those was written for a 40-year-old woman, and which was written for an 18-year-old? The class should have no difficulty at all in identifying which is which, because the dialogue matches the character.

Back in Chapter 3 we suggested to the children that listening to what people around them say could be a useful source of story ideas – and *listening to how they say it* can be equally valuable in helping them become good writers of dialogue. The way people speak can say a lot about them. If we hear people giving their opinions on radio phone-in programmes, we start to build up a mental picture of them, despite the fact that we can't see them. The language that they use, and the way that they use it, can give us all sorts of clues to their personality: are they clever? Not very bright? Pompous? Humorous? Aggressive? Nervous? We tend to form opinions of them, even though we don't know them – and it's all based on their vocabulary and delivery.

So if we use our ears and become familiar with the way that pompous or humorous or aggressive or nervous people speak, then we'll be able to write very realistic dialogue for a character who has those personality traits. Listening is the key – that's why it's called having a good ear for dialogue!

Telling a story through scenes

A play, a film or a television programme is a story told through a succession of scenes, *each of which should have a purpose*. That may sound obvious, but sometimes young people have a tendency to write scenes full of polite exchanges between characters – 'Hello, how are you?' ... 'I'm fine thanks, how are you?' ... 'I'm good. What do you fancy doing today?' ... – which ramble on without really getting anywhere, and hardly move the plot along at all.

Scenes should be there for a reason – to tell us something about the situation and characters, fill in the Back Story or progress the plot – and by the end of them the audience should know more than they did at the beginning. To make sure that is the case, young writers should do some preparation work before starting to write their script. They will find it helpful to go through their story outline, with its journey and obstacles, identify the key moments in the plot and note them down as bullet points. Each of these bullets could be a scene by itself, or it might be covered in two or more scenes, or multiple bullets could be combined in a single scene. Whichever is the case, they will have a template for telling their story in scenes.

If we treated the story of Cinderella in this way, it would look something like this:

- Set up Cinderella's character and situation.
- The invitation to the ball arrives.
- The Wicked Stepmother and Ugly Sisters try to prevent her going.
- She needs a ball gown – Fairy Godmother provides it.
- She needs a carriage – Fairy Godmother comes to the rescue.
- She gets to the ball and dances with the Prince.
- The magic stops at midnight – she has to flee.
- The Prince finds the slipper.
- The search to find its owner ends at Cinderella's house.
- The Wicked Stepmother and Ugly Sisters attempt to stop Cinderella trying it on.
- The slipper fits her and the Prince proposes.
- The wedding.

In the Disney film there are additional scenes – notably featuring the comic mice – which are there mainly for entertainment purposes. However, they all contribute to the plot in some way: for example, there is a funny scene in which the mice make Cinderella a dress using materials 'borrowed' from the Ugly Sisters, which ultimately leads to heartbreak for our heroine when the Sisters claim them back; and there are comic battles with the cat, which become significant towards the end of the film when he becomes an obstacle to them rescuing Cinderella. *All* the scenes – even the ones that seem to be included just to provide comedy – have a purpose. And that should be true of the children's scripts as well.

They should try to include as much action as possible in each scene, so that the story unfolds in a visual way; if scene after scene consists solely of conversations between the characters, the audience are unlikely to be kept on the edge of their seats. It's worth telling the class, if they don't know already, that back in the far-off days of silent films, stories were told without any dialogue at all. We may not want them to go quite that far – especially since we've shown them the importance of writing good dialogue! – but left to their own devices, children tend to include too many conversations and too little action, and their scripts suffer because of it. Refer them to those scenes from Disney's *Cinderella* in which the mice are making a dress or battling with the cat: maximum action – minimal dialogue.

First steps in scriptwriting

Writing a full script involves a lot of work and can be a daunting task. I would suggest that they begin their scriptwriting careers by writing *three scenes only*. They could take a story which they have already written as prose and adapt it as a script, or they could think of a completely new story. Whichever is the case, they should focus on three scenes which follow on from each other:

1. A short scene which tells the audience something about the Main Character and situation.
2. The scene in which the Inciting Incident occurs.
3. A scene in which the Main Character faces his or her first obstacle.

This should not be too difficult a task, and the resulting short script should contain enough incident and drama to make it entertaining, even if it is not telling a complete story. Having practised the basic skills of scriptwriting in this way, they can then go on to complete the script at a future date if they (and you) wish.

They will, no doubt, want to see their scripts performed – and that will be a hugely beneficial lesson in itself. Just as reading dialogue out loud is the one sure way of finding out if it sounds authentic, so putting a script to the test by performing it is the only way of telling if it works and seeing how it might be improved. All in all, the classroom could be a pretty noisy and lively place during this lesson!

14

Advanced scriptwriting

If they can write good dialogue and structure a story in scenes, as outlined in the previous chapter, young people should be able to write perfectly service-able scripts and get a lot of pleasure from doing so. But older or particularly gifted pupils may not be satisfied with turning out a serviceable script; they may have ambitions to write something a bit more sophisticated, something that has more depth – in which case there are some additional things that it would be useful for them to know.

Whether we are writing a story or a script there will be things we have to tell our audience so that they know what is going on: information about the situation, the Back Story and the plot that is unfolding. We will need to tell them things about the characters: what kind of person they are, and what they are thinking and feeling about the things that are happening around them. This is what is known as exposition – and in prose it is relatively straight-forward. In a script, however, it is more difficult.

Some of the essential information can be given to the audience by means of dialogue between the characters, but how do we convey a character's innermost thoughts and feelings? In this chapter, we'll be looking at how this can be achieved through *non-verbal communication*, by getting the class thinking about *body language*, and by casting some light on the mysteries of *subtext*. We will also be giving the class some tips on the *structure of scenes* and showing how – rather surprisingly – some of the things they've learned about non-fiction writing can be useful in that respect.

Non-verbal communication

We all use *body language* to communicate things without words. Most of the time we do it unconsciously – but scriptwriters should be *very* conscious of non-verbal communication. The more clues they can give to an audience about a character's thought processes, the better. Give the class this example of how a person's body language can show what is going on in their mind:

The scene is a small convenience store. Four schoolchildren enter and start to browse the shelves – and the shopkeeper never takes his eyes off them for a moment, even moving further down the counter so that he has a clearer view of them. *What is he thinking?*

Obviously, he's worried that the children might steal something, and he wants to make sure that they don't. Through his actions we can read his thoughts.

Now try the class with two more examples – and, if possible, persuade a couple of volunteers to perform them. In my workshops I have found that getting pupils to play the characters and act out the suggestions of their class-mates can be very instructive – not to mention highly entertaining. Here's the first scenario:

A man has just been visited by a detective who came to speak to him. It's not important *what* the detective had to say – that would depend on the plot – but what we *are* interested in is how the visit has affected the man. As he closes the door, how would we show the audience his mental state? Ask the class what gesture or action might show that he felt:

1. Angry?
2. Nervous?
3. Relieved?

Get them to imagine how *they* might react to the detective's visit. What would someone normally do under those circumstances? How do actors in films, plays or television programmes convey anger, nervousness or relief?

Hopefully, they will come up with a variety of things the man could do; for example:

1. If he was angry, he might slam the door, or punch the wall or kick a pair of trainers that were lying in the hall.
2. If he was nervous, he might bite his lip, heave a worried sigh, his eyes might flicker from side to side as he wonders what to do. He might go to the window and look out to make sure the detective has gone.
3. If he was relieved, he might close his eyes and give a deep sigh. He might mop his brow. He might flop down in a chair as if all the strength has gone from his legs.

When you have exhausted the possibilities of this scenario, try a second one: a woman receives a letter and sits down to read it. The audience don't know what it contains, and we're not going to tell them. But we *do* want to give them a clue – so how do we show that it is:

1. Good news?
2. Bad news?
3. Infuriating news?

Perhaps the class might come up with these reactions for the woman:

1. She smiles as she is reading it – that's easy!
2. She suddenly freezes as she is reading; her mouth drops open; she may allow the letter to drop from her fingers as she stares distractedly into space; she might blink away tears.
3. She may purse her lips in anger, give an angry snort or crumple the letter in her hand.

Probably they will come up with quite a few more. But now that we've got them thinking about body language, we're going to complicate things a little, by introducing them to …

Subtext

This is a term that encompasses a number of things, including the underlying theme or message of a play or film, which may not be stated explicitly; meanings or character traits that are *inferred*. Not an easy concept for young writers to get their heads around, and one which they probably don't have the skills to master at this stage. But one form of subtext that they *should* be able to handle can be summed up in this way: *characters say one thing – but really they mean something different.* And this gap between what is said and what is meant can be a very useful way of showing what a character is thinking.

The best way to illustrate this to the class is by giving them some actual examples, so get them to picture this scene:

A young couple – very ordinary-looking, wearing jeans – walk into a posh jewellery shop to buy an engagement ring, and start to look at some very expensive ones in a cabinet. The man behind the counter says in a patronising tone, 'We've got some lovely ones just down here that I think you might like', and guides them towards a cabinet further down the counter which is full of much cheaper rings. *Does he really mean that the rings he's steering them towards are lovely? Or is he saying something else?*

What he's really saying to them is: 'Those other rings are far too expensive for you. These are much more in your price-range.' He may even think they might want to try on one of the valuable rings and then do a runner with it.

What he says and what he means are two different things – and because of that, the audience has been given an insight into his thought processes and his personality. He's prepared to take the couple's money off them, but deep down he doesn't really want them in his shop. He's a bit of a snob who would rather be dealing with richer, posher customers. We haven't *told* the audience that – we've *shown* them. And that's why subtext can be so useful to a scriptwriter.

Subtext can also be combined rather well with body language, as this little scene shows:

Two women – let's call them Sally and Jane – are chatting in the living-room of a house, and Sally is monopolising the conversation. Yak, yak, yak … it seems as if she'll never stop talking and Jane is bored silly. How do we know this? Easy – through her body language. She keeps inspecting her nails and glancing at the magazine that lies open on the sofa next to her, reading bits of it surreptitiously. She hardly looks at Sally at all; she's not paying attention. She could, of course, tell Sally to give her jaw a rest – but that would be out of character for Jane. She's kind and thoughtful and – even though she talks too much – Sally is her friend and she doesn't want to offend her. So what does she do?

Well, she suddenly pretends that she has heard a noise, says to Sally 'Was that the doorbell?', gets up and leaves the room. A few seconds later, she returns, saying 'I must have been mistaken.' By her action, she has stemmed the flow of Sally's relentless conversation – if only for the time being! What she said wasn't what she meant – but if we were the audience, we would know why she said it, we would have known what was going through her mind, and we would have learned that she was a tactful and kind-hearted person.

Young writers are not going to become experts in body language and masters of subtext overnight – but if they are made aware of them, then they can start to watch out for examples of these forms of communication in any films, plays or television programmes they may watch: *How is the heroine letting us know that she dislikes the man she is talking to? Why do I know that the detective suspects the gardener?* By studying how actors – and the professional writers who created the scripts – convey thoughts and emotions, they can pick up tricks and techniques that they will find useful in their own writing.

If you wish to set the class a *writing exercise* to cover what they have learned, get them to write this scene from a film or play:

Setting: The customer service desk in a clothing store.

Characters: A young, rather cheeky female shop assistant and a pompous, aggressive, middle-aged woman customer.

Situation: The customer is returning a dress that she bought last week, complaining that the seam split the first time she wore it and demanding her money back. The shop assistant doesn't believe the woman's explanation: it looks to her as if the dress has been worn several times – and there is a stain on it that looks suspiciously like white wine. She thinks the dress is probably too small for the woman anyway, and that the woman went to a party in it, started dancing too energetically, and the dress split. But, of course, she can't say that – she has to be polite to the customer.

Style: Probably quite humorous.

Suggest to them that they try to use body language and subtext to show that the shop assistant doesn't believe the woman, even though she can't say so. And tell them to remember this:

When we are writing scripts, we must always remember that the audience doesn't know as much about the character, the situation and the plot as we do. We must constantly ask ourselves things like: 'Will the audience understand what the character feels about what has just happened? How can I make it clear to them? How can I *show* them?' There's an old saying that actions speak louder than words – and that could be the scriptwriter's motto.

Scene structure

As mentioned in the previous chapter, each scene of a play or film should be there for a reason, such as moving the plot along, giving information or providing further insights into a character. And in order to serve this purpose effectively, it needs to be structured properly. In particular, *it needs to end well.*

A good general rule for young writers to follow is to build a scene up towards a dramatic moment, such as a piece of action or an important revelation – and then end it as soon as possible afterwards. In a nutshell, it's:

1. Set the scene.
2. Deliver the message.
3. Job done – get out of there.

In a murder story, for example, we might see a woman arriving home to find the house empty – and it shouldn't be. Where is her husband? She searches the house, room by room, calling his name. She arrives at the bedroom, opens the door ... and finds him lying in a pool of blood. She screams – and that's where we should end the scene. Do we really need to see her rushing to the body, checking for a pulse, racing downstairs and phoning the police? No – the purpose of that scene is to establish that the man has been murdered. Once the body has been found, it's mission accomplished – move on.

Not all scenes end as dramatically as that, of course – otherwise the stage or film set would be littered with dead bodies. But we can't just let a scene meander along and then dribble out – there should be something significant about the way it ends, something that excites the audience or intrigues them, something that makes them want to know what happens next and lures them into the next part of the story.

So how do we achieve that? Well, in previous chapters, we've seen that there's a fair bit of cross-over between different forms of writing – and here's further proof: two of the non-fiction endings given in Chapter 8 can also be very useful for ending a scene, either individually or combined. They are:

1. Add a final piece of information.
2. Hint at further developments in the story.

Add those to the big dramatic incident and you have three excellent ways of bringing a scene to an end – not the only ones, of course, but very effective ones. Examples of these three types of scene endings can be found frequently in plays and films – but a particularly rich source of examples is TV soap operas. How many times have we witnessed scene endings like these?:

■ The argument in the pub gets out of hand; the first punch is thrown and a full-blown fight ensues (dramatic incident).

■ 'I've got something to tell you, Duane. I'm pregnant!' (final piece of information + hint at further developments).

■ 'You've had long enough. I want that money *tomorrow*, or else ...' (hint at further developments).

They all provide 'cliff-hanger' moments that make the audience want to keep watching. So now we know that strong scene endings are important – but what about the start of scenes? We've neglected those so far, for the very good reason that *scene openings are less crucial than endings*.

At the very start of a piece of drama, the writer needs to grab the audience's attention in some way, so that they are drawn into the plot. But we don't need to keep on doing that at the start of every subsequent scene because – hopefully – the previous scene will have ended with a dramatic moment or revelation that will have made them eager to find out what happens next. As the next scene begins, there is no need to 'hook' them, because they should already be hooked. In fact, it can often be a good idea to start the next scene quite gently and un-dramatically, so that the viewers have time to digest what has just happened, before we give them something new to think about as we build up towards the next climax.

Structuring scenes in the way we have shown will give a good rhythm and flow to the script – dramatic incidents and moments of intrigue following one after the other, with quieter moments in between, like waves crashing on the shore, receding and then returning. And all building up inexorably towards a climax at the end. Good scene structure results in good scripts – and that's what every writer, young or old, is aiming for.

Non-fiction – advanced

15

Advanced non-fiction techniques

In Chapter 8, when dealing with the subject of writing to inform, we got the class to focus on how to begin and end their journalistic piece, with the section in between – the main body of the story – just being filled in as bullet points. Now we are going to return to that same story and give our full attention to *the middle section*, showing the class how to assemble disparate pieces of information into a logical and coherent flow.

This will entail re-using two of the worksheets supplied in the Teacher resources section:

- Jacob Brown facts.
- Jacob Brown press release.

In addition, the class will need the intros and endings to the Jacob Brown story that they wrote during the Chapter 8 workshop. If they don't have them to hand, then they will need to write new ones – which is maybe not a bad idea anyway, since the more practice they have at writing openings and endings, the better.

We will also be looking at *what type of information is needed* for this type of story, and discussing the difference between a *news story* based solely on facts and a *feature article* in which the writer can express his or her opinions.

The middle section of a news story

We have emphasised time and again the importance of strong openings and endings in both fiction and non-fiction writing – but, of course, the way in which we get from the one to the other is vital, too. After all, the middle section makes up the major part of a piece of writing, and if we don't fully engage our readers' attention during it, we run the risk of losing them before they even get to the end. If the middle is disjointed and hard to follow, they may decide part-way through that they don't want to carry on reading, and go off and do something else instead. There is far less danger of that happening if the piece is readable and flows smoothly, so let's see how we can achieve that by looking again at **Jacob Brown facts**:

JACOB BROWN FACTS

1. Jacob Brown is 18 and comes from Leeds. He is a 6th former at Allerton Grange School.
2. Jacob belongs to Leeds City Athletics Club and competes in the triple jump and long jump.
3. He used to play basketball, but took up athletics three years ago.
4. Last weekend he won a triple jump gold medal and a long jump bronze medal at the North of England Championships held in Sheffield.
5. When he competed in the triple jump last year, he didn't qualify for the final.
6. His winning distance in the triple jump was 14.50m (his personal best is 15.20m) and in the long jump he achieved 6.46m (personal best 7.46m).
7. On Tuesday, Jacob was asked to bring his medals to the Allerton Grange 6th Form Assembly, where his triple jump winning distance was marked out in string, and his schoolmates congratulated him.
8. When Jacob was interviewed, he said: 'Even though I won, I didn't jump as well as I could. But it's early in the season and I'm hoping to get better.'
9. Jacob's ambition is to become the national champion, and then to qualify for the Commonwealth Games. The Commonwealth Games trials are in June this year, and the qualifying distance is 16m.
10. Jacob said: 'I think I can get it right in time, and if I do, representing my country at the Commonwealth Games would be a great experience. I'd give it my best shot, and hopefully my best might be worth a medal.'

Distribute the document to the class and point out to them that the information falls into three categories:

■ Details of two events – the medal-winning performances and the school assembly (facts 4 and 7);
■ Background information – Jacob's age, school, athletics club, personal best times, how long he has been jumping, other sporting activities, ambitions, etc. (facts 1, 2, 3, 5, 6 and 9);
■ Quotes (facts 8 and 10).

This information will need to be presented in a clear and logical sequence that tells the story in an entertaining and informative way. To help the flow of the story, they should look to see if any of the separate pieces of information can be linked in some way so that one leads naturally to another. For example:

- Mentioning which school he attends might link to the assembly where he showed his medals.

Ask the class if they can find any other potential links. Some that they might come up with are these:

- Mentioning his athletics club could be linked to the information about how long he has been an athlete and the fact that he previously played basketball.
- His quote about not jumping as well as he could might be linked to details of his winning distances and personal bests.
- Alternatively, his winning distances might be linked to the fact that they were marked out in string at the school assembly.

So now we have some idea of how the information will flow; we have an intro and we know how we will end the piece (hopefully!). Now comes the moment of truth. It's time to write the full story.

The class should be aiming to write about half to three-quarters of a sheet of A4. Depending on their age and ability, and whether they are working singly or in teams, they should be allowed anything up to three-quarters of an hour – plus time added on afterwards for them to read out their efforts and compare the effectiveness of the various approaches they may have taken.

At the end, it may be instructive to look at the way in which I wrote the story for the local newspaper – the document entitled **Jacob Brown press release**.

LEEDS SCHOOLBOY ATHLETE IS NORTH OF ENGLAND CHAMPION

Young Leeds athlete Jacob Brown was jumping for joy at the weekend when he was crowned junior triple-jump champion at the North of England Championships held in Sheffield. And yesterday his fellow 6th Formers at Allerton Grange School in Moortown celebrated his success at a special assembly.

Jacob's winning jump of 14.50m was marked out in string across the school hall, and his schoolmates crowded round to admire the gold medal he won in the triple jump, and his bronze medal awarded in the long jump.

Even with two medals in the bag, Jacob wasn't totally satisfied with his performance at Sheffield. The distances he jumped in both events were below his personal best but, as he said, 'It's still early in the season, and I'm hoping to get better.'

A member of Leeds City Athletics Club, 18-year-old Jacob only took up athletics three years ago, but already he is making a name for himself. At last year's North of England Championships he didn't even make the final, and his two-medal haul this year shows just how quickly he is improving.

Now his sights are set on higher things: firstly on becoming national champion, and then on qualifying for the 2006 Commonwealth Games. The triple jump qualifying mark of 16m is just 80cm beyond his personal best, and he is hopeful that he can make the improvement before the Commonwealth Games trials in June this year.

'I think I can get it right in time', he says, 'and if I do, representing my country at the Commonwealth Games would be a great experience. I'd give it my best shot, and hopefully my best might be worth a medal.'

While the class are reading it, get them to identify the type of opening, the type of ending, and any examples of linked information that they might spot. Analysing press stories in this way is something they can do every time they look at a newspaper – and seeing the same types of intros and endings used time and time again should convince them that the techniques and structures you have taught them are the ones that 'proper' journalists and writers use!

Gathering information for a story

In the case of the Jacob Brown story, all the facts and information the students needed were provided in the sheet they were given. But if they were writing a story from scratch, they would obviously need to gather the facts themselves – and this is how they should set about it:

If you are interviewing someone in order to get the details of a story, you need to get as much information as possible. You should imagine that you were going to be quizzed about it afterwards by a very demanding sub–editor – would you be able to answer any question that might be put to you?

First, you need to find out the basics:

- What happened?
- Who was involved?
- When did it happen?
- Where did it happen?

- Why did it happen?

With that information, you have the bare bones of your story – now you need to put some flesh on the bones by acquiring:

- Every scrap of information you can get about the event itself.
- Any background information and details that might be useful.
- Quotes from the person or people involved, expressing their feelings, opinions and reactions to what happened.
- Quotes from any other relevant source – witnesses, officials, experts, etc.

Having done that, you will have a list of facts and quotes similar to the list provided for the Jacob Brown story. Then all you have to do is identify the Key Point, decide how you will begin and end, look for potential links that will help the story flow – and you're ready to write. It sounds like quite a 'to-do list', but this process soon becomes second nature to writers: with a bit of experience they find themselves doing it all automatically.

Feature articles

Feature articles are different from news stories in several respects: like a news story, they are usually informative, but sometimes there is also an element of entertainment to them. News stories deal in facts, while in a feature article, the writer will often give his or her personal opinion about something. For instance, if a school magazine included a story about a forthcoming school trip, including details of when the trip was happening, how many pupils would be going, what the destination was and some of the activities planned for the children when they got there, then that would be a news story, concerned solely with facts. If, in the next edition of the magazine, a pupil wrote about his or her impressions of the trip – 'It was the best ever' ... 'my favourite bit was ...' etc., then that would be a feature article.

Fact and opinion are two different things – and the writer's opinion should never creep into a news story. Sadly, this golden rule is all too often ignored in some of the more strident and partisan newspapers, where good journalistic standards are sometimes sacrificed in pursuit of the newspaper's own agenda. End of lecture.

However, since young people are more likely to be writing feature articles than hard news stories – informative but entertaining pieces for the school magazine or for a website, for example – then they will usually be free to give full rein to their thoughts and opinions. They will also find that the ways of beginning and ending a piece that they have learned will continue to serve them well – and since feature articles often have a lighter and more entertaining tone than news stories, they will find the Tease Opening and the Circular Ending (if they can pull it off) particularly effective.

If the article they are writing is a particularly long one, composed of several different elements – for example, a feature for the school magazine on 'Life in the Sixth Form' or a tribute to a teacher who is retiring after 40 years at the school – then the standard non-fiction structure may need some slight adaptation.

In the examples given, the articles would not be telling one story, they would be telling several: 'Life in the Sixth Form' would probably be a collection of different case studies to illustrate a variety of courses and ambitions; the tribute might well be a succession of incidents and recollections to illustrate the veteran teacher's career.

The secret of writing articles such as these is to think of the different elements as separate stories, each with their own internal structure – a comparable approach to the one outlined in Chapter 14, when we discussed the structure of individual scenes within a script.

In a feature article which contains multiple elements, young writers might find it helpful to identify the Key Point of each separate one, and give them all their own intro and ending. The different elements can then all be linked together in one long article which has its own over-arching Key Point ('The Sixth Form caters for a wide variety of people' or 'Mr Charlesworth has made an enormous contribution to the school'), its own intro and its own ending.

Hopefully, young people will find the structures and techniques outlined in this book helpful when they are thinking about what to write and how to set about it, and during the act of writing itself. They are guidelines only, and not intended to be prescriptive – the last thing I would want to do would be to tell a young writer that they *must* write in a certain way. Plenty of highly successful writers bend and break the 'rules' and produce brilliant work, but in many ways they are like the tightrope walkers who amaze the audience by dancing or skipping or doing hand-stands on the high wire: before they were able to do that, they had to learn to do the basics, like walking from one end of the wire to the other, without falling off. And so it is with writing.

Only when young people have absorbed and mastered the basic skills of writing are they fully equipped to experiment with them, find new and dazzling ways of enthralling their readers and make their own contribution to the ever-developing craft of writing. And wouldn't it be wonderful if some of the pupils who have taken part in our workshops and lessons went on to do just that?

PS Did you notice what I just did there? That was a 'hinting at further developments' ending, proof – if it were needed – that the things I've written about in this book actually work. 'Ah', you might say (if you were being pernickety), 'but in adding that PS, you've given the book a new ending so now it *doesn't* hint at further developments after all.' And that's true – but it *does* 'add a final piece of information'. Covers most eventualities, this writing technique business, doesn't it?

Teacher resources

WHO IS THIS CHARACTER?

- What is his name?
- How old is he?
- What is his family like?
- What sort of house does he live in?
- What does he do in his spare time?
- What are his likes and dislikes?
- Is he clever?
- Is he popular, with lots of friends?
- What sort of school does he go to?
- Do you like him or dislike him? Why?
- Is he adventurous?
- What would he like to be when he grows up?
- Why would readers identify with him?
- Give me one surprising fact about him.

WHO IS THIS CHARACTER?

- What is her name?
- How old is she?
- What is her family like?
- What sort of house does she live in?
- What does she do in her spare time?
- What are her likes and dislikes?
- Is she clever?
- Is she popular, with lots of friends?
- What sort of school does she go to?
- Do you like her or dislike her? Why?
- Is she adventurous?
- What would she like to be when she grows up?
- Why would readers identify with her?
- Give me one surprising fact about her.

GREEN DAY ROCK THE LEEDS FESTIVAL

_____ guitar playing by Billie Joe Armstrong and _____ drumming from Tre Cool sent the crowd wild as Green Day's _____ musicianship stole the show at the Leeds Festival. The atmosphere was _____ as the _____ threesome put together the most _____ set imaginable, starting with their _____ new single 'American Idiot', and winding up with Queen's _____ 'We Are the Champions'. The performance was _____ from start to finish. _____ gig. _____ band!

GREEN DAY ROCK THE LEEDS FESTIVAL

_____ guitar playing by Billie Joe Armstrong and _____ drumming from Tre Cool sent the crowd wild as Green Day's _____ musicianship stole the show at the Leeds Festival. The atmosphere was _____ as the _____ threesome put together the most _____ set imaginable, starting with their _____ new single 'American Idiot', and winding up with Queen's _____ 'We Are the Champions'. The performance was _____ from start to finish. _____ gig. _____ band!

AWESOME	AWESOME
AWESOME	AWESOME
AWESOME	AWESOME
AWESOME	AWESOME
AWESOME	AWESOME

BRILLIANT	BRILLIANT
BRILLIANT	BRILLIANT
BRILLIANT	BRILLIANT
BRILLIANT	BRILLIANT
BRILLIANT	BRILLIANT

INTROS AND ENDINGS

The Key Point of the story:
'A 10-year-old girl has become the youngest person ever to swim the Channel.'

****

TWO WAYS TO START A PIECE OF WRITING

1. **The Key Point Opening.**
2. **The Tease Opening.**

The Key Point intro:
'At the age of just 10 years and 3 months, Brighton schoolgirl Hayley Wyngarde has become the youngest person ever to swim the Channel.'

The Tease intro:
'Brighton schoolgirl Hayley Wyngarde meets up with her friends every weekend to go swimming at the local leisure centre.

But last Saturday, she was unable to join them; Hayley had an important swimming engagement elsewhere – in the English Channel.

And by Sunday morning she had become the youngest person ever to swim from Dover to Calais – at the age of just 10 years and 3 months.'

FIVE WAYS TO END A PIECE OF WRITING

1. End on a quote.
2. Remind your readers of the Key Point/sum up.
3. Add a final piece of information.
4. Hint at further developments in the story.
5. The circular ending – referring back to your opening.

Ending on a quote:
Hayley said: 'Two miles out from Calais I was feeling so tired that I was tempted to give up. But I kept on going – and now I'm really glad I did. Beating the world record is something I've always dreamed of.'

Reminding readers of the Key Point/summing up:
A spokesman for the Distance Swimming Association said: 'Swimming the Channel is an enormous challenge, even for the most experienced swimmer. To achieve it at the age of 10 is a remarkable feat.'

Adding a final piece of information:
Hayley beat the record set by French boy Lucien Rius, who was 10 years and 11 months old when he swam the Channel in 1997.

Hinting at further developments:
When she's had time to recover, Hayley will begin training for her next challenge – she's planning to swim the 36km length of Loch Ness later this year.

The Circular Ending (if Tease Opening is used):
Hayley is determined to join her friends at the leisure centre next weekend as usual, because the staff there have laid on a special treat for her – a party to celebrate her world record.

WHAT TYPE OF INTRO AND ENDING?

1

REF'S CHOCOLATE PUDDING BRIBE

Top referee Mike Riley told Allerton Grange students about the closest he ever came to being offered a bribe: "I was refereeing at a school," he said, "and they offered me a free dinner with chocolate pudding!"

Mike was holding a question and answer session with a group of 6th Form and GCSE P.E. students, after giving them a presentation about the art of refereeing as part of a drive to encourage more young people to pursue referee training courses. The group of quizzed him about such issues as shirt-waving celebrations, diving, video replays and the best goals he'd ever seen, as well as that bribery issue.

Afterwards, Mike renewed his acquaintanceship with our own former top-flight referee, Kevin Lynch. Mike said:

"Talking to kids in schools really gives me a buzz. They've got so much enthusiasm: it reminds me of what I was like at that age." Mr Lynch, on the other hand, probably can't remember that far back!

By the way, if you want to read the inside story of what it's like being a top referee, get your hands on a copy of Mr Lynch's book Lynch the Ref! – out now.

2

LANGUAGE NO BARRIER

Less than two weeks after its world premiere at the West Yorkshire Playhouse in June, a play in English and Mandarin Chinese was performed to an audience of Year 7 students at Allerton Grange at the start of a tour of six Leeds schools.

The Dutiful Daughter, a story of love and conflict set on the Isle of Joy, is the result of a collaboration between the WYP Touring company and the Sichuan People's Art Theatre. Two actors from the Chinese theatre take the lead roles of the princess and the fisherman she loves.

The play's director, Gail McIntyre, said that having some of the dialogue in Chinese was not a problem for an audience of schoolchildren. "Unlike an adult audience, children are not bothered if they don't understand every word," she said. "They get the meaning from the visuals."

Arts Liaison teacher Terry Ram said: "It's a great privilege to have real theatre in schools; the children are able to get really close to the performance and talk to the actors afterwards. We are thrilled to have been involved with this project."

3

WHIZ KIDS

A team of Allerton Grange students has taken the fast track to success by winning two trophies in the Formula One Challenge, a national contest to design and build aerodynamic model racing cars.

The six-strong team used computers in the school's Technology department to design and cut the model cars from blocks of wood, and then raced them against 15 other teams from West Yorkshire in a speed trial at the White Rose Centre, using carbon dioxide canisters to propel the cars along a 25 metre track in under a second. Our team won the trophies for Fastest Car and overall Best Team, and will now be taking part in the national finals of the competition.

WHAT TYPE OF INTRO AND ENDING?

4 WORKHOUSE BOY MAKES GOOD

From workhouse boy to the West End stage and back to the workhouse again - former pupil Andrew Gowland's career path may read like something out of a cheap novel, but it's true - well, in a way! For the brilliant actor whose first appearance on the Allerton Grange stage was in Oliver! returned to the school in June to help with the latest production .... Oliver!

One of the most gifted performers ever to tread the boards at Allerton Grange, Andrew's first chance to shine came in 1991, when he was a Year 7 student with a burning passion for the theatre. He auditioned for Oliver! and was offered the part of .... workhouse boy number five! He must have made a big impression, though, because from then on his rôles in school productions got bigger and bigger: good parts in Carousel and West Side Story, and leading rôles in Threepenny Opera, Little Shop of Horrors, Cabaret and Annie Get Your Gun.

After leaving Allerton Grange, Andrew travelled throughout South East Asia before taking up a scholarship at the Birmingham School of Speech and Drama, where he specialised in musical theatre, spending part of his course studying in the USA. After graduation he acquired a West End agent and began his career as a professional actor, which included being one of the London cast of Murderous Instincts at the Savoy Theatre on the Strand.

After being offered a post-grad place at the Royal Academy of Music, starting in September this year, Andrew decided to put his acting work on hold for the summer, which gave him the opportunity to return to the scene of his earliest triumphs.

When he heard that Allerton Grange were preparing to stage Oliver! again, the former workhouse boy number five offered his services as production assistant - an offer which the Drama department was thrilled to take up.

So how does it feel to be back? "Fantastic!", according to Andrew. "I had such a blast when I was here that I didn't want to leave. It's such an amazing school for drama."

5 BIG BROTHER COMES TO ALLERTON GRANGE

...But don't worry! This isn't a story about young exhibitionists behaving badly on TV – it's about a brilliant new Aim Higher initiative for immersing students in a foreign language and bringing some fun to end of term language teaching.

The Big Brother house, complete with diary room, was recreated in the City Learning Centre, and pupils from 14 different schools checked in to hang out together, draw up a shopping list for the food they were likely to need and tackle various tasks set out for them by Big Brother. It was just like the TV programme, but with one big twist – nobody was allowed to speak in English.

When our own group of Year 9 & 10 students entered the house in July, the language of the day was French, and the task was to write and perform a song or rap for Eurovision. The Big Brother running the show was Catriona McLeod, the CLC's languages project co-ordinator, aided and abetted by three native French speakers.

Catriona, who speaks Spanish and German as well as French, said she was very impressed by the language skills and enthusiasm of the students. She added: "Fun events like this really encourage the students, and hopefully leave them with good memories of languages. Most of the students who took part will go on to study the language at GCSE."

6 TAYABAH THE HIGH FLYER

Year 7 student Tayabah Ahmed's perfect attendance record at school has made it certain that she's going to be a high flyer – because it has won her a trip in the Radio Aire helicopter.

Tayabah won the dream flight in "Give It 100%", a 96.3 Radio Aire competition to encourage school attendance. More than 20,000 Leeds schoolchildren with a 100% attendance record during March were entered in a draw for a wide range of prizes, including walkmans, i-Pods and events tickets, and Tayabah was the lucky winner of the Logiecopter Experience, which will see her flying 1500 feet above the city during the radio station's breakfast show and helping to provide traffic reports. Other prize winners from Allerton Grange were Khola Ilyas of Year

7, Chelsee Hendrickson from Year 8, Year 9's Antony Lamprey and Elliot King-Davies plus Yuan Yuan Hu and Simon Harris of Year 10.

Presenting Tayabah with the star prize in a ceremony at the school, Radio Aire Drivetime presenter Cameron Prudames said: "As a big part of the local community, we always like to get involved in campaigns like this. We really connect with young people – and being able to use our influence with them to encourage good attendance at school is a really worthwhile thing to do."

And Tayabah's thoughts on her forthcoming flight? "I'm going to be a bit scared", she said, "but it's really exciting!"

JACOB BROWN – facts for a Press Release

1. Jacob Brown is 18 and comes from Leeds. He is a 6th former at Allerton Grange School.
2. Jacob belongs to Leeds City Athletics Club and competes in the triple jump and long jump.
3. He used to play basketball, but took up athletics three years ago.
4. Last weekend he won a triple jump gold medal and a long jump bronze medal at the North of England Championships held in Sheffield.
5. When he competed in the event last year, he didn't qualify for the final.
6. His winning distance in the triple jump was 14.50m (his personal best is 15.20m) and in the long jump he achieved 6.46m (personal best 7.46m).
7. On Tuesday, Jacob was asked to bring his medals to the Allerton Grange 6th Form Assembly, where his triple jump winning distance was marked out in string, and his school-mates congratulated him.
8. When Jacob was interviewed, he said: 'Even though I won, I didn't jump as well as I could. But it's early in the season and I'm hoping to get better.'
9. Jacob's ambition is to become the national champion and then to qualify for the Commonwealth Games. The Commonwealth Games trials are in June this year and the qualifying distance is 16m.
10. Jacob said: 'I think I can get it right in time, and if I do, representing my country at the Commonwealth Games would be a great experience. I'd give it my best shot, and hopefully my best might be worth a medal.'

PRESS RELEASE

LEEDS SCHOOLBOY ATHLETE IS
NORTH OF ENGLAND CHAMPION

Young Leeds athlete Jacob Brown was jumping for joy at the weekend when he was crowned junior triple-jump champion at the North of England Championships held in Sheffield. And yesterday his fellow 6th Formers at Allerton Grange School in Moortown celebrated his success at a special assembly.

Jacob's winning jump of 14.50m was marked out in string across the school hall, and his schoolmates crowded round to admire the gold medal he won in the triple jump, and his bronze medal awarded in the long jump.

Even with two medals in the bag, Jacob wasn't totally satisfied with his performance at Sheffield. The distances he jumped in both events were below his personal best but, as he said, 'It's still early in the season, and I'm hoping to get better.'

A member of Leeds City Athletics Club, 18-year-old Jacob only took up athletics three years ago, but already he is making a name for himself. At last year's North of England finals he didn't even make the final, and his two-medal haul this year shows just how quickly he is improving.

Now his sights are set on higher things: firstly on becoming national champion, and then on qualifying for the 2006 Commonwealth Games. The triple jump qualifying mark of 16m is just 80cm beyond his personal best, and he is hopeful that he can make the improvement before the Commonwealth Games trials in June this year.

'I think I can get it right in time', he says, 'and if I do, representing my country at the Commonwealth Games would be a great experience. I'd give it my best shot, and hopefully my best might be worth a medal.'

SOUTH ASIAN TSUNAMI FACT-SHEET

- A tsunami is a series of giant waves.
- Tsunamis are often caused by earthquakes or the eruption of volcanoes.
- The South Asian Tsunami struck on 26 December 2004.
- It was caused by an underground earthquake in the Indian Ocean.
- The earthquake which triggered the tsunami registered between 9.1 and 9.3 on the Moment Magnitude Scale.
- It was the second largest earthquake ever recorded.
- The waves of the tsunami were up to 25 metres high.
- The tsunami devastated many countries on the coasts of Asia and Africa.
- Indonesia, Sri Lanka, India and Thailand suffered the worst damage.
- Malaysia, the Maldives, the Seychelles, Kenya, Somalia and Tanzania were also affected.
- Almost 300,000 people were killed and many more were injured.
- 242,000 died in Indonesia, 31,000 in Sri Lanka and 16,000 in India.
- It was one of the worst natural disasters of all time.
- As the waves hit, families were separated from each other, with parents unable to hold on to their children.
- Throughout the region, children were left searching for their parents.
- Many children were orphaned.
- Thousands of families were left homeless and lost their livelihoods.
- Schools were destroyed, making a return to some sort of normal life more difficult for the children.

BEGINNING AND ENDING – Tsunami Story

TWO WAYS TO BEGIN:

Key Point Opening:
A massive tsunami swept across the Indian Ocean today, devastating coastal areas and causing thousands of deaths.

Tease Opening:
It was just another Sunday in the Indonesian city of Banda Aceh: people going about their business, children playing on the seafront, fishing boats bobbing in the harbour.

But in less than a minute, people, boats and buildings were all swept away by an 18-metre wall of water as the tsunami struck.

FIVE WAYS TO END:

Reminding readers of the Key Point:
With thousands of people dead and communities destroyed in many countries around the Indian Ocean, the tsunami was one of the worst natural disasters of all time.

Adding a final piece of information:
The earthquake which triggered the tsunami registered between 9.1 and 9.3 on the Moment Magnitude Scale, making it the second largest earthquake ever recorded.

Hinting at further developments:
As the scale of the devastation became clear, governments around the world promised help for the stricken region. A 150-strong UK medical team will be flying out to Indonesia today, with more aid teams to follow in the next few days.

The Circular Ending:
It began just like any other Sunday – but as evening fell, the people of Banda Aceh who were lucky enough to survive knew that they had witnessed a day that none of them would ever forget.

Ending on a quote:
The utter devastation wrought by the tsunami was summed up by one local, when he said: 'There used to be streets here – now there's nothing but rubble and mud. I saw a wrecked car wedged in the branches of a tree and a fishing boat dumped on the roof of a house. It was just like a nightmare.'

THE TSUNAMI CHILD
SOME QUESTIONS TO ASK YOURSELF

- What is his/her name?
- How old is he/she?
- What did he/she lose?
  - Mother?
  - Father?
  - Both parents?
  - Brothers/sisters?
  - Home?
  - School?
- What happened to him/her *during* the tsunami?
- Was he/she injured?
- What happened to him/her *after* the tsunami?
- How can donations of money help him/her?
  - Rebuild the family home?
  - Rebuild the town or village?
  - Support an orphanage?
  - Rebuild a school?
  - Provide food?

INDONESIAN NAMES

Boys:

Budi	Chahaya	Dian	Jegan
Kersen	Pramana	Ramelan	Setiawan

Girls:

Arti	Atin	Endah	Kade
Lastri	Merpati	Sujatmi	Tuti

SRI LANKAN NAMES

Boys:

Anishka	Bandula	Dilip	Gihan
Iranga	Marvan	Roshan	Padman

Girls:

Amanthi	Dayani	Gayesha	Hashini
Manisha	Nanda	Nayana	Vidu

INDONESIAN NAMES

Boys:

Budi	Chahaya	Dian	Jegan
Kersen	Pramana	Ramelan	Setiawan

Girls:

Arti	Atin	Endah	Kade
Lastri	Merpati	Sujatmi	Tuti

SRI LANKAN NAMES

Boys:

Anishka	Bandula	Dilip	Gihan
Iranga	Marvan	Roshan	Padman

Girls:

Amanthi	Dayani	Gayesha	Hashini
Manisha	Nanda	Nayana	Vidu

Index

3-act structure 100, 104–5
advertising 75–6
Alan Bennett 74–5, 109
antagonist 91, 97, 102–4
anti-hero 97
Awesome resource 61–2, 134

back story 10, 19–22, 36, 48, 91;
    exercise 93–4; in scriptwriting
    111, 114
Beginning And Ending – Tsunami Story
    resource 72, 81, 143
beginning, middle and end 45, 57,
    78–80, 104
body language 114–8
Brilliant resource 61–2, 135

character journey 7–10, 22, 25, 29,
    32, 44–5, 48; in Cinderella 11–16,
    25; in Harry Potter 17; multiple
    journeys 100–5
character names 35, 37–8
Cinderella: Back Story 19–21, 36,
    93; beginning of 45–6;
    denouement 105; dilemma
    exercise 98; ending of 48;
    motivation exercise 96–7; parallels
    with Harry Potter 17; parallels

with King Lear 28; point of view
    49; protagonist v. antagonist
    exercise 103–4; Seasons structure
    in 107–8; sequel exercise 21–6;
    scene breakdown 112; structure of
    8, 10–16
cliff-hanger 119
coincidence 25
conflict 97, 102
Cool Runnings 100–1, 105
creating characters 26, 37, 40–3,
    91–3, 99

delayed drop 66 *see also* Tease
    opening
denouement 104–5
dialogue 109–12
dilemmas 91, 98–9

endings, fiction 44–5
endings, non-fiction 57, 64, 67–9,
    81–2, 83–5, 125–8; add a final
    piece of information 67–9, 71, 81,
    129; circular ending 67–9, 71, 81,
    85, 128; end on a quote 67–9, 82;
    hint at further developments
    67–9, 71, 81, 129; remind readers
    of the Key Point/sum up 67–8,

71, 81, 83; resource 137; uses in fiction writing 101, 119; *see also* intro

engaging the reader's attention 45, 85

exposition 109, 114

fact versus opinion 127

False Horizon 7, 14–18, 22–3, 33, 44, 104

feature articles 123, 127–8

goal 9–12, 22, 103

Green Day Rock the Leeds Festival resource 61, 133

Harry Potter 9–10, 17–18, 92

headline 78–9

imagination 75–6, 78, 80

Inciting Incident 7, 12, 16, 18,103–4, 113; and story openings 46–8; in Cinderella sequel exercise 22–3; in Harry Potter 17; in story creation 31–3, 44

Indonesian & Sri Lankan Names resource 74, 79, 145

interviewing 126–7

intro 66, 68, 71, 125–6, 128

Jacob Brown facts resource 64, 70–1, 123–4, 140

Jacob Brown press release resource 72, 123, 125–6, 141

Key Point 62, 64–7, 69–71, 83–5, 127–8

linking information 125–7

listening 27, 29, 111

main character 7–8, 12, 22, 97, 113; creating 40–3; readers identifying with 10–11,16, 44, 46, 91; *see also* protagonist

middle section 57, 64, 71, 78, 81, 85, 123–4

motivation 24–6, 91, 95–7, 100–1, 103

Mrs Doubtfire 94–5, 105

news story 65, 70–2, 81, 123–8; differences from feature article 123, 127

non-fiction writing 57–9, 62–3, 67, 114, 123

non-verbal communication 114–16

observant 27, 29–31

obstacles 11–18, 22–3, 101; characters as source of 91, 97, 102–3; in story creation 32–3

Obstacles structure 7, 12, 16, 19, 94; and 3–act structure 100, 104

Odd One Out 29–30

openings, fiction 44–8

openings, non-fiction 57, 64, 66–7, 69, 81, 83–5, 125–8; Key Point opening 66–7, 69, 81, 83, 85; Tease opening 66–7, 69, 71, 81, 85, 128

outlines 19, 22–6, 49, 52, 95

outsiders 10

pay-off 79

pitching 65

plagiarism 28

point of view 44, 49–50

protagonist 8, 22, 91, 97, 100, 102–4; *see also* main character

repetition 59–62
research 73, 82, 84
rewriting 51–3
Robin Hood 94

scenes: endings of 118–20; openings
of 119–20; structure of 114,
118–20, 128; telling a story
through 109, 111–12
Seasons structure 100, 105–8
sentence length 62–3, 87
set-up 24, 79, 91, 94–5
showing not telling 109, 118
situation 21, 46, 104, 111–114,
117–18
South Asian Tsunami Fact-Sheet
resource 72, 74, 76–7, 80, 142
statistics 87
stereotypes 35, 38–40
story structure 7, 10, 57, 108–9
storylines 23, 26, 98
style 87
subtext 109, 114, 116–18
sympathetic characters 11, 95

targeting writing 58–9, 67, 80
The Hobbit 8–9
The Lord of the Rings: antagonists 97;
character journeys 8, 102;
character names 38; character
motivation 95; denouement 105;
False Horizon 15; well-rounded
characters 92
The Simpsons 91–2
The Tsunami Child resource 74,
78–9, 144

under pressure 98–9
'Unexpected' technique 27, 31, 33

variety of language 58–60
villains 29, 38–9, 52, 97; see also
antagonist
visualising 75, 77, 109
vocabulary 58, 60–2

What Type of Intro and Ending
resource 69, 138–9